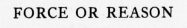

FORCE OR REASON

LONDON : HUMPHREY MILFORD

OXFORD UNIVERSITY PRESS

FORCE OR REASON

ISSUES OF THE TWENTIETH CENTURY

BY

HANS KOHN

PROFESSOR OF HISTORY, SMITH COLLEGE

CAMBRIDGE, MASSACHUSETTS

HARVARD UNIVERSITY PRESS

1937

First Printing, February, 1937
Second Printing, June, 1937

PRINTED AT THE HARVARD UNIVERSITY PRESS
CAMBRIDGE, MASS., U.S.A.

To

WILLIAM ALLAN NEILSON

WHO AS A MAN, A SCHOLAR, AND A LEADER SETS TO THE
YOUNGER GENERATION THE EXAMPLE OF A TRUE
LIBERAL AND A TRUE HUMANITARIAN

PREFACE

THIS short book is based on three lectures delivered in July, 1936, at the Summer School of Harvard University under the title "Three Fundamental Issues of the Twentieth Century." They have been enlarged and annotated for publication. I wish to thank Professor Kirtley F. Mather, Director of the Summer School, and Dr. Dumas Malone, Director of the Harvard University Press, for their friendly and encouraging interest, the staff of the Smith College Library for their unfailing courtesy, and Miss Eleanor Ernst for her conscientious assistance in preparing the text and the notes for publication.

H. K.

Northampton, Mass.
   August, 1936

CONTENTS

FORCE OR REASON

O genus humanum, quantis procellis atque iacturis quantisque naufragiis agitari te necesse est, dum bellua multorum capitum factum, in diversa conaris. Intellectu aegrotas utroque, similiter et affectu. Rationibus irrefragabilibus intellectum superiorem non curas, nec experientiae vultu inferiorem, sed nec affectum dulcedine divinae suasionis, cum per tubam Sancti Spiritus tibi affletur: 'Ecce quam bonum et quam iocundum, habitare fratres in unum.'

— DANTE, *De Monarchia*, Liber I, finis.

INTRODUCTION

THE object of this book is to analyze briefly some of the aspects of the post-war world and to try to trace their historical background. The different factors in our present situation are, of course, not unknown and they are necessarily treated here with a brevity which does not allow us to follow all their ramifications and implications, both as regards their origins and motivations and as regards their consequences. I have tried to draw attention to their interrelation and to interpret them, as far as that is possible in a chaotic world, with some coherency. In fact there seems to me amidst all the complexity today less chaos in the world than is generally assumed.

In contemporary treatises we come again and again across a tone of defeatism when the great aims of the American, French, and Russian revolutions are mentioned — freedom and equality of all men and peoples. Those aims were certainly not realized by the revolutionists; nevertheless their efforts left a deep and growing impress on the mind of man and produced durable and expansive changes

in society. The world today is not "safe for
democracy," but democracy is today much
stronger in the world than it was in the year
1900. Nothing is as misleading as the statement frequently encountered that so many
democratic states have abandoned democracy
since the World War. The shortsightedness of
these statements is amazing. Some states
which after the World War accepted democratic paper constitutions which had no roots
in the social or intellectual traditions of those
countries have to a certain extent changed
their constitutions to a closer agreement with
the traditions which until the World War had
dominated their life. But even this changed
status has frequently marked a very definite
progress compared with the pre-war consti-
tutional life or with pre-war participation of
the masses in politics. All those countries of
Europe, moreover, in which democracy was
rooted in the social and cultural life in 1900
have not only remained democracies but have
strengthened their democracy — Great Britain, France, Belgium, Holland, Scandinavia,
and Switzerland. They have broadened the
suffrage and in most of them Socialist or Labor parties have for the first time in history
occupied the seats of government. New re-
cruits have been won to the democratic ranks

in countries where democracy is still young and
therefore precarious — in Finland, Czechoslovakia, and Spain. Even in those countries where democracy is feeble, disputed, or
still in the travails of birth, there is today undoubtedly more democracy than in 1900 —
in all parts of the former Russian Empire, and
in the Balkans, where attempts at personal
dictatorship by kings and generals meet with
a growing resistance by a nascent peasant
democracy. Prussia and Hungary were not
democracies in 1900 and are not today. The
only country in which democracy has lost, as
compared with the many gains elsewhere
since 1900, is Italy, but there democracy was
not yet sufficiently rooted in the social structure and intellectual life of the country. In
the large parts of the Old World outside
Europe we witness everywhere today struggling democracies where in 1900 they were entirely unknown and even undreamt of. Before them lies a long and painful process of
transformation, but it turns undoubtedly in
the direction set by the examples of the pio-
neer movements of the nineteenth century.

Thus we do not believe that the achievements of the nineteenth century are lost in the
twentieth, but we know they are no longer
sufficient. From the American and French

revolutions to the World War we were moving by a slow process and through a long struggle towards a state of society which can be described as national democracy in the progressive countries, the benefits of this democracy being largely, although diminishingly, confined to the upper and middle classes. The problem presented to the twentieth century is the enlargement of democracy and all that it implies, liberty and equality, dignity and happiness, in two directions: internationally, to embrace all peoples, those which are progressive and those which are backward, in a coöperative federation; socially, to arrive at equal opportunity for all men and all classes. This task will be infinitely more difficult than even that accomplished in the nineteenth century. It will suffer many disappointments and long setbacks. It will demand far greater effort and struggle than the preceding step demanded. It will demand serious and hard thinking and whole-hearted devotion, since the greatest obstacles will be offered not only by vested sentimental and economic interests but by inveterate tendencies in all of us.

Nevertheless, the seriousness with which these questions are asked today is a hopeful sign. Modern civilization is not a function of science and technique, of greater efficiency and speed; it is a human attitude which can be resolved into two main components — a living and active social conscience, a sense of responsibility and willingness to help man as man; and an objective search for truth in the pursuit and application of which group and individual interests and emotions are as far as possible eliminated. The immense and unprecedented difficulties of modern civilization make it the greatest venture and adventure in human history. It is a challenge thrown out to the coming generations of the twentieth century. The historian of the twenty-first century will record their response.

THE CULT OF FORCE

καλόν κατάρξασθαι φιλίας, καὶ τῷ τῶν ἠτυχη-
κότων ἐλέῳ σπείσασθαι τὴν διαφοράν. δεῖ γὰρ
τὴν μὲν πρὸς τοὺς φίλους εὔνοιαν ἀθάνατον
φυλάττειν, τὴν δὲ πρὸς τοὺς ἐναντίους ἔχθραν
θνητήν· οὕτω γὰρ συμβήσεται τοὺς μὲν συμ-
μάχους γίνεσθαι πλείους, τοὺς δὲ πολεμίους
ἐλάττους.
— Diodori Bibliotheca Historica,
Liber XIII, 23, 1.

CHAPTER I

THE CULT OF FORCE

THE generation which lived through the World War and the troubled years of its aftermath has gained a new understanding of history. It has lived through the first great general upset since the wars of the French Revolution and of Napoleon. Europe had enjoyed one hundred years of a comparative peace and of a comparatively undisturbed social and intellectual development. The wars fought during those one hundred years were mostly distant colonial wars or wars of very short duration and involving generally only two or three countries. They brought with them political changes of a limited territorial scope, but scarcely far-reaching social or intellectual transformations.[1]

The World War was entirely different, by reason of its length, its scope, and its consequences. Our generation which has lived through the Russian Revolution and the ensuing civil war understands the different phases of the French Revolution much better than our fathers could. We can see today what the generations of 1815 to 1850 could not see, how definitely and profoundly the French Revolution has changed political thought and social order. Figures like Robespierre, the Terror and the Counterterror, no longer appear to us who have witnessed the post-war transformations in Europe so strange and unique, nor so inhuman as they did in the nineteenth century. We have seen in our own day fanatics stranger than Robespierre and terror and regimentation carried much further than anything the Convention could dream of. But we recognize today Robespierre and Charles X only as accelerating or retarding elements in the unbroken progress of the consequences of the French Revolution. The courageous fight for liberty which Charles James Fox carried on in the House of Commons in his day against the Treason and Sedition Bills of Pitt's government will be judged by us, who have come to value the worth of liberty from very recent experiences, with greater understanding and sympathy than it was by the Victorians, who were so secure in their knowledge of the untrammelled progress of liberty.

Progress, liberty, romanticism — what different connotations and melodies are today in these words: doubts, dimmed hopes, dark forebodings and anxieties which were undiscerned by the generations immediately preceding ours. Do not many of us today better understand and view differently the intention of the Holy Alliance[2] and the policy of Castlereagh, the achievements of Bismarck and the failures of Napoleon III?[3] The consequences of the Industrial Revolution and of the unprecedented accumulation and expansion of capital confront us in a way unsuspected by those who lived through their early stages. We see the shortcomings of the nineteenth century with almost painful clarity, but do not our times, when in some quarters all the achievements of the French Revolution and of the nineteenth century are vilified and questioned, make those achievements appear to us in a new light and rekindle in many the love for liberty and reason, which a generation ago we all took for granted and therefore almost disregarded, forgetting that generations had labored, fought, and died to achieve them and make them secure?

Dazzled by the bright picture of the progress of rational and liberal humanism in the nineteenth century, the generation at the turn of the century often overlooked or failed to appreciate the portentous consequences which some of the tendencies, which had made themselves felt as the nineteenth century drew towards its end, would have in the future. Since then, three of those tendencies have become the dominant issues of our own time: the Cult of Force, the Dethronement of Reason, and the Crisis of Imperialism seem today to determine the political, intellectual, and social life, at least in large parts of Europe and the Old World.

They have threatened least, perhaps, to become a dominant issue in the United States, and this circumstance seems to me to give a unique importance to the United States at the present time. It was the first country in the world to found its whole political life on the principles of the age of rationalism and enlightenment embodied in the Bill of Rights; it does not carry on the traditions of an aristocratic or absolutist past which so largely determine the life and outlook of the people in Germany and Russia; a military caste and a standing army never played any important role in America's social and political life. The very fact that the people of America are immigrants coming from many different countries and from diverse racial stocks — but finding in America a common promised land of a freedom unknown in their home countries — leads towards an emphasis on elements common to all of them. There seem to me more of a reasoned humanism and a social Christianity in American intellectual life than in any European country. It is perhaps because America is such a young country and was entirely built on the foundations of the eighteenth century in the nineteenth century that the nineteenth century proves here so strong a mold, that America is so much less affected by the crisis than is the rest of the world.[4]

For the crisis today is not only and not even mainly an economic one. It is a general crisis, or, to use a modern word, a totalitarian crisis, embracing the whole man and the whole life of society — its intellectual foundations, its social order, its economic structure, and its political forms. The crisis is even a totalitarian crisis in another sense: it is the first crisis in the history of the world which is not confined to a few countries or to a continent. It has made itself felt — in all its aspects, intellectual, social, economic, and political — as well in China as in India, in Africa, and in Europe. In this way it is unique, for the Renaissance and the French Revolution were totalitarian crises of a similar intensity, but of much smaller extent: large parts of the earth were not touched by them. Today we witness everywhere a reshuffling of the patterns of life, a search for new standards and new systems, a deep unrest.

Again the United States seems to me less affected than other countries. Therefore it is here today that we are both allowed to discuss all the aspects of the crisis with full liberty and that it is incumbent upon us to do so, because we are enough involved in the crisis to understand it and distant enough from its emotional confusion to analyze it and to gauge its consequences. America has carried infinitely less of the burden of the World War and of its aftermath than other countries. The comparative isolation of the United States gives it a more detached perspective of the crisis of our century than other parts of humanity enjoy.

If we try to describe the civilization of the nineteenth century, the period which started with the American and French revolutions,[5] there is no other civilization in history with which we could compare it except, in some respects, the ancient Attic civilization. Both are secular civilizations with man at their center. The eighteenth century brought about in the intellectual life of Europe the dechristianization of western humanity.[6] Man ceased to look up to heaven and did not regulate his life any more in view of a life beyond. Theology lost the central position which it had reoccupied after the short interlude of the Renaissance in the periods of the Reformation and Counter-Reformation. Man did not concentrate his intellectual efforts any more upon defining God and his attributes or upon expounding the Holy Scriptures. Man looked upon the earth as his real abode. He trusted in reason and science as his guides. The new age was, as in ancient Athens, an age of humanism, of confidence in man as the center of all things, of his right and his power to order this world according to his wishes and his abilities, to secure for him and his fellow men the new goods to which he felt himself entitled: life, liberty, and the pursuit of happiness. Unbounded horizons seemed to open before man, his reason seemed able to penetrate them.

The nineteenth century went in some fundamental aspects beyond Attic civilization. Its rationalism divested itself of the rhetorical element which seemed inseparable from ancient civilization, and became factual, based upon experience and first-hand research. The proud patriotic feeling of the citizen of the ancient *polis* with his rights and responsibilities again animated the people, but the representative system allowed for its application far beyond the narrow limits of the city to which it had been necessarily confined in ancient Greece. Finally—an inheritance from Judaism and Christianity — the idea of progress introduced a new dynamic force into civilization and in its secularized form made man the conscious builder of humanity's future.

This civilization believed in Man and Reason, in the human and in the reasonable, in what the Greeks had praised as *sophrosyne*. Reason was common to all normal men: it was therefore possible to arrive by rational explanations and by discussion at a reasonable settlement of all disputes. In a world ordered by reason the application of force still remained necessary, but it was to be used only as far as it was strictly unavoidable. It was recognized as an evil which had its justification in the still existing but diminishing imperfection of man and of society. Force had to be strictly controlled both in the frequency and in the manner of its application, which were hedged around with all possible precautions. The development of the state in the nineteenth century, the state based on the Rule of Law, tended to confine force and violence to exceptional cases, both within the state and in the relation between states. Force still remained in the background as an *ultima ratio*, but it was regarded as unfortunate to be obliged to have to take recourse to it, and it was done only when all other arguments had failed. As far as men and governments used force, they did it with a bad conscience.

This temper has changed since the World War. During the War, force became legitimate, not only in the relations between states but even within the state. Everywhere civil liberties and the right of free discussion were curtailed or suspended. Men learned to divide their fellow men into friends and enemies. The foremost political theorist of the present German government, Carl Schmitt,[7] has defined politics as based upon the inescapable antagonism between friend and enemy as ethics are based upon the antagonism between good and bad and aesthetics upon that between the beautiful and the ugly. Political conflicts are those in which existence itself is at stake and in which war and extermination are always postulated as a guiding and real possibility. This friend-enemy relation (in the original German the well-sounding alliteration of the words *Freund-Feind*

Verhältnis makes us more easily overlook the fallacies contained in the argument) has to be recognized and accepted, and it is the state which decides in its sovereignty who is the enemy. But politics meant in Athens and meant during the nineteenth century something different: not to acknowledge an inescapable friend-enemy relation, but to avoid such a relation, or if it arose to try by good politics to avoid its aggravation and to smooth it away. There is certainly a primitive instinct in man to regard an adversary or anyone in the way of his desires and aspirations as an enemy, an implacable foe who has to be exterminated. Civilization and statesmanship consisted until recently in finding the ways and the means to overcome the primitive instinct by law, by compromise, by every effort at a peaceful and friendly settlement.

Professor Schmitt's theory is born in the intellectual climate of the World War. It would however be only a philosophical curiosity were it not that it represents a very widespread post-war attitude. Force has come to be regarded as a great master-builder. Patience and compromise are laughed at. People do not try to convince their adversaries, to solve patiently difficult problems. They "liquidate" their enemies. They solve problems in

the same way that Alexander the Great loosed
the Gordian Knot: by cutting it. Force
again seems to give to the master man or to
the master people the supremacy of the
world. In this sense Chancellor Hitler could
speak of "the victorious sword of a master
people which brings the world into the service of a higher culture."[8] Only a generation
ago this close combination of sword and culture would have sounded even in Germany
stranger than it does today.

Right and law protect the weaker, force
opens the way for the stronger and the more
powerful. Simultaneously with the new cult
of force, the cult of the strong man and the
strong nation arise. At the beginning of the
nineteenth century a man stands out who
sets the great example for the coming superman. Napoleon is without doubt the most
astonishing phenomenon in world history.
Perhaps Alexander the Great could be compared to him, but Alexander was a descendant
of kings and his father had already marked
out his kingdom clearly for a still greater future. Napoleon's astonishing career was
wholly his own work, not only unaided by
precedent or station in life, but in complete
opposition to and disregard of all traditional
order and custom. In breaking with all the

traditions of his time Napoleon was the first
solitary man, alone against the whole world,
strong only with his own force, relying only
upon himself. There seemed no limit set to
his march through life and to his decisions
except his own daring and his confidence in
himself. The ambition and the uniqueness of
a powerful ego growing and expanding without consideration for others, the greatness of
the overbearing strong man, were first crys-
tallized in his person. He dared to challenge
fate like Prometheus, not in order to bring
fire down from Heaven to warm all the weaker
brethren and to make life easier and happier
for them on earth, but for his own glorification and in order to lord it over others. Napoleon has deepened our knowledge and
understanding of the potentialities of men.
Friedrich Nietzsche, who took up the idea of
the superman, could point out that "Napoleon represents the passion of new spiritual
possibilities, of an extension of the soul's
domain." He made the army the instrument
of his will to power. He transformed the wars
of the eighteenth century, which had consisted mainly of a long-drawn-out evasion of
battles, into sharp and short conflicts with the
aim of striking as decisively and as unspar-
ingly as possible the death blow to the enemy.

In the early history of the nineteenth century Napoleon was the lone meteor. The influence of his example was felt only in literature, in the titanic romanticism of a whole generation. In life, however, the ideas of the nineteenth century, common sense and moderation, dominated an age which its detractors belittle today as "bourgeois" and which certainly did not claim to be "heroic." In France itself the bourgeois sense of order and balance, the Hellenic tradition of harmony and the humane, led to a complete repudiation of Napoleon and the titanic spirit of unbridled ambition. His name has no magic spell in France as that of Frederick the Great has in Prussia. Statues to Napoleon or streets named in his honor are extremely rare in France.

It was, however, in Germany that this titanic romanticism found its fiercest expression, there not only as a deification of the individual ego, as with Napoleon, but of the superindividual national genius. In England this romanticism was represented on a national basis only by lonely thinkers like Carlyle, who, with his stress upon the power of personality and of moral intuition as embodied in the Teutonic race, his glorification of might as right and of the rule of the strong, tried to transplant German romanticism to England. Only towards the end of the nineteenth century did the cult of force become a practical issue in politics, and since then many little Napoleons, with their unmeasured aspirations, their love for a heroic fullness of life (at the possible risk of self-destruction, but certainly at the risk of destruction or degradation of the weaker), with the identification of indomitable strength with goodness and of outward greatness with worth, have become characteristic of our time.

There is however a fundamental difference between the lonely superman at the beginning of the nineteenth century and the many supermen and supernations of our time. Even Napoleon regarded force and war not as goods in themselves but as a transitional means of achieving a peaceful humanity, a unified world empire of equal races and men such as Alexander the Great had set out to create. Today we have made great progress in the cult of force beyond anything Napoleon could have dreamed. A peaceful world is regarded as impracticable and even undesirable; force and war are believed to be forever necessary and salutary elements of life without which peoples decay. There can be no equality between strong races and weak ones, between supermen and — a new discovery of our time — undermen or submen, weaklings who are only good enough to bless a kind fate which put the supermen above them. The most authoritative statement of the philosophy and faith of Fascism, the article which the head of the Italian government contributed in 1932 to the *Encyclopedia Italiana* on "The Political and Social Doctrine of Fascism," contains the following passages: "Above all, fascism, the more it considers and observes the future and the development of humanity quite apart from political considerations of the moment, believes neither in the possibility nor the utility of perpetual peace. It thus repudiates the doctrine of pacifism, born of a renunciation of the struggle and an act of cowardice in the face of sacrifice. War alone brings up to its highest tension all human energy and puts a stamp of nobility upon the peoples who have the courage to meet it. This anti-pacifist spirit is carried by fascism even into the life of the individual; the proud motto of the squadrista, '*me ne frego*,' written on the bandage of the wound, is the summary of a doctrine not only political — it is the education to combat, the acceptation of the risks which combat implies, and a new way of life for Italy."[9]

Fascism, Signor Mussolini goes on to explain, "affirms the immutable, beneficial, and fruitful inequality of mankind" without disclosing what the standard of measurement is for ranking men. But it is clear from the whole context that this criterion is force, power, might. Therefore the highest expression of human life is the highest expression of human power: empire. Thus the aim of Fascism can be defined as empire, which Mussolini calls "an essential manifestation of vitality," and Fascist education as education of the people into an army which will combat for and conquer an empire to be ruled by a superior race under the leadership of a superman.

Mussolini could have quoted Nietzsche's famous aphorism from his *Will to Power*: "In this age of universal suffrage, in which everybody is allowed to sit in judgment upon everything and everybody, I feel compelled to reëstablish the order of rank. Quanta of power alone determine rank and distinguish rank: nothing else does."[10] Nietzsche is claimed today as a forerunner by Fascists and National Socialists. The official organ of the Hitler Youth Movement bears the significant title *Wille und Macht* ("Will and Power"). Nietzsche's personality is much too deep and much too complex to be claimed by any one political or intellectual movement. He was too much of a strong individualist, too much of a hater of the state — the "coldest of all monsters" — to be appropriated by Fascism; too much of a lonely thinker, too contemptuous of racial theories and of nationalism, to be claimed by the National Socialists. But he undoubtedly was an apostle of a new morality, or rather amorality, of force and power. His philosophy was so daring that the depth and implications of his new morality were barely understood in his lifetime and did not exert any influence outside a small circle of intellectuals.

Much more widespread than the influence of this individualistic titanism was that of the nationalistic titanism of Wagner with its romantic idealization of racial myths and of pre-Christian barbaric heroism, strangely tempered — and this is what Nietzsche could not forgive him — with Christian ideas of renunciation and holiness. The doctrine of force, however, became of practical importance not through Wagner and not through Nietzsche, but through Bismarck.

Bismarck is sometimes acclaimed as the leader in the unification of the German nation; but Bismarck was not a German nationalist. He did not hesitate to ally himself with Italy against Austria, which was then a predominantly German state and a leading member of the German Confederation. He did not hesitate to incite the Slav Czechs, the Jugoslavs, and the Hungarians against Austria and against the German supremacy of Austria. He was first and foremost a Prussian and he looked for the aggrandizement of Prussia and for her liberation from Austrian hegemony. Prussia had been a great state before Bismarck. Bismarck made her the leading power in Europe.

Prussia originally was a very poor country with very little fertile soil, lacking natural resources, culturally the most backward part of Germany, a land which had been colonized and won over from the Slavs only during the later Middle Ages. The great electors and kings of the house of Hohenzollern succeeded by a remarkable feat in converting this poor country without any natural frontiers, with long borders, difficult to defend, into a powerful state by the concentration of all the moral, intellectual, and economic resources of the country upon the building up of an army. The army became the center and the life-blood of the state; the soldierly virtues set the example for the citizen; a highly trained and

efficient, incorruptible bureaucracy guided
the people with paternal care in the ways of
discipline and in reverence for those higher
up, for the uniform of the King, for the ideals
of the state. The great and lonely genius,
Frederick II, full of contempt for men, used
his excellent army as a tool for his enlight-
ened ambitions. It is even far more useless to
claim Frederick II for German nationalism
than Bismarck. Nothing was farther from his
imagination than a German nationalism. Culturally he was French and a cosmopolitan;
politically he allied with non-Germans against
Germans and Germany; but he perfected the
method and instrument by which Prussia
was to become the leader in Germany and by
which it was even to grow to European hegemony under Bismarck: the army and its
spirit.[11] Although this army was shattered to
pieces in 1806 at Jena, its spirit survived. Within a few years Scharnhorst, Gneisenau, and
Clausewitz had created a new army which,
later perfected by Roon, Moltke, and King
William I himself, became the powerful instrument which made it possible for Bismarck
in three short wars, within seven years, to
constitute Prussia the most powerful state in
Europe and to put upon the head of his royal
master the imperial crown.

National movements had agitated Europe during the first half of the nineteenth century. The aims of those national movements were to free the people from despots, to secure popular freedom. Their leaders were moved by generous humanitarian ideas: they were nationalists, but at the same time they dreamed of a peaceful humanity of fraternal nations living each in freedom and respecting the freedom of its neighbors. The nationalists were united in an informal international alliance. They fought together on the various national battlefields; their cause was the common cause of liberty and humanity. These sentiments animated not only the fighters of 1848 but even Napoleon III, although his weak and vacillating personality never allowed him a clear-cut policy.

A turning point in the temper of nationalism had come, however: the unification of Italy and of Germany was not accomplished by the nationalists of 1848. Cavour and Crispi, not Mazzini and Garibaldi, the army and diplomacy, not the people, realism, not idealism, secured the unification of Italy. The genius of Bismarck, comparable in German history only to that of Frederick the Great, through masterful diplomacy and the help of that unique instrument of power, the Prussian army, created not a free Germany but a powerful Germany.

The victory of Bismarck, achieved in the teeth of the opposition of German liberalism, not only marked a turning point in German history and the complete defeat of the ideals of 1848 in Germany: its importance reached far beyond. Bismarck's diplomacy and the Prussian army were admired throughout Europe and set an example. The ideals of the first half of the nineteenth century, liberty and independence, were replaced by new ideals which may be summed up in the words dominion and power. Imperialism became a conscious movement, agitating the masses, and Rudyard Kipling became the popular poet and writer in England.

In November, 1859, in the same year in which Cavour started by unscrupulous diplomacy the unification of Italy, Charles Darwin had published his epoch-making volume, *On the Origin of Species by Means of Natural Selection or the Preservation of Favored Races in the Struggle for Life*. Soon his biological theories were applied to sociology. Life, not only in nature but also in history, seemed a permanent struggle for existence. The result of this struggle was, to use Herbert Spencer's phrase, the survival of the fittest.

Man and history lost their spiritual meaning;
they were only part of an immense biological
naturalistic process — a great tragedy — in
which, as everywhere in nature, the stronger
prevails and therefore is the best, best fitted
for the exigencies of life. The powerful needs
no justification for his conquests. Nature
affords the justification; it is beyond good and
evil; it is inescapable. History is thus a permanent struggle and the world belongs to the
stronger. That is nature's law, proved by
science, the highest guide of the new humanity. The strong was able to use force
without a bad conscience any more. He
needed no conscience; what mattered was
only success. As Darwin published his *Descent of Man* in 1871, the same year in which
Bismarck completed his unification of Germany by the might of a victorious army, the
battle which had raged in educated circles
about the theories of evolution had been decided. The masses were now ready to receive
the new gospel. From now on, God in the
popular imagination was with the stronger
battalions, with the more highly developed
technique of destruction.

If God had been dethroned in the eighteenth century, the later nineteenth century
dethroned man. Man was no longer the voli-

tional center of the universe, he seemed no more than a cog in the immense machine of nature, subject to the laws of natural selection as all other animals and plants. He had to shoulder the tasks which nature imposed upon him, willy nilly. He had to bear the white man's burden or to fulfill and obey the manifest destiny of his race in the history which appeared as a struggle of races.

As it took a long time to draw the ultimate conclusions from the dechristianization of western humanity,[12] so it took a long time to feel the consequences of the dehumanization of western mankind. Before the World War the faith in man and reason was still too strong, liberal and socialist theories were too widely held, too deeply ingrained in the intellectual life, to be replaced by any extreme conclusion drawn from the new cult of force and success. Only the solitary genius of Nietzsche saw deeper, recognized the fundamental crisis of all the traditional moral values, and had the courage to draw the conclusion which seemed at that time absurd and fantastic.

The new cult of power and success, the fact that every self-esteeming nation considered as its right and duty expansion and rule over others, necessarily was bound to lead to ever-

growing conflicts. One of the strangest facts
to a historian of recent times is that the majority of the people in Europe and America
seemed surprised by the coming of the World
War, although since the seventies everything
had pointed towards the coming catastrophe.
The preparations, both material and mental,
had grown from year to year, but so strong
still was the inheritance of the nineteenth
century, the faith in man and reason, that it
seemed hardly believable that something so
unreasonable and so inhuman as a large-scale
war could happen. It was overlooked that
wars had gone on since 1870 almost without
interruption, but they were wars in Asia or
Africa, distant colonial wars which seemed not
to count. It was overlooked likewise that
since 1871 threatened alarms of war had been
not infrequent in Europe, but again there
seemed a tremendous difference between play-
ing with the possibility of war and letting the
war dogs themselves loose.

Pacifists speak often of the horrors of war
as a deterrent. There is undoubtedly much
truth in this. Modern warfare with its all-
dominating mechanization seems to dispel
much of the ancient glamour of primitive
soldierly heroism. In most countries and in
most armies men who did not do their duty

in the hinterland were threatened with the
punishment of being sent to the front.
Death for the Fatherland was apparently not
regarded as sweet and glorious, but as befit-
ting malefactors.

Nevertheless we should not forget that
many young men in most countries welcomed
the war. It seemed to them, at least at the beginning, a liberation from the daily dull rou-
tine of their lives, an escape from mediocrity
into something glamorous, from drab offices
into the great world, full of excitement and
adventure. The great magician of the Italian
language, Gabriele d'Annunzio, had glorified
in his novels and poems in the last decade
before the World War the thrills of aviation,
the spirit of record-making sport, of modern
gladiators. Under his influence war appeared
as a supreme fulfillment, as a unique intensifi-
cation of life. With some literati, who nevertheless influenced part of the intellectual
youth, the craving for heroism became a com-
pensation for the lack of faith. Benedetto
Croce, himself not entirely without some responsibility for this new spirit, characterizes
as the ideological reflection of "industrialism
and Bismarckism, an uneasy condition of
mind, a combination of frantic craving after
power, restlessness and withal lack of enthusi-

asm and indifference."[13] These literati, a small but vociferous group in all countries, had lost faith in God and faith in man. Would they find a new faith, a new reality which seemed to them worth living for, in the horror and excitement of war?

The decisive objection against war seems to me not to lie in its physical horrors but in its human degradation. War in itself is opposed to the spirit of liberalism and democracy, not because men are killed and maimed, but because there does not exist any other situation in which by necessity the freedom and dignity of man, the autonomous display of his moral judgment, and the equality of men are so thoroughly abolished and suspended as in war. Strict discipline without critical reasoning or questioning, undisputed and practically unlimited and infallible authority, the ready acceptance and application of force and brutality, are the indispensable fundaments on which alone a war can be waged, especially a modern war with its huge masses of men involved.

A short or a distant war may not affect very deeply the intellectual and moral outlook of those who participate in it. In any case their number is small. The World War lasted for over four long years, longer than the period which we apply to the education and character building of the youth of military age in our colleges; it was fought in the heart of and all over Europe; it involved practically the entire populations of the belligerent countries and affected the life of the people even in the few neutral countries. It is easy to understand that the experience of the generation which had spent long and decisive years in the trenches or in the atmosphere of the trenches put a lasting stamp on the succeeding years.

Many found, in rebellion against the degradation of man in war, a new faith in man, a new liberalism or socialism. This happened mostly in those countries where the traditions of the eighteenth and early nineteenth centuries, their rational humanism, are deep-rooted and strong — in France and Great Britain.[14] It was different in the Central European countries — in Germany and Italy. Many of the young men who returned from the experience of the trenches carried with them what was called the *Fronterlebnis* of the generation into the hinterland. Those four years had after all been their youth, the great experience of their life, not devoid of the memory of good comradeship. On their return home they were greeted by the shouts of "No more

war!" Their own great experience, their
sacrifices, were regarded as futile. The war
seemed a failure, not only politically and
economically. They had to justify their own
existence, the four years which were the core
of their life. They had to glorify their life in
the trenches and with it the spirit of war and
the virtues of the soldier.

For this generation force was no longer a
moral issue to be debated: it was the natural
outcome of life. The Prussian spirit was revived, but this time without all those restrain-
ing influences which religion and rationalism
had exerted on it under the great Hohenzollern and Bismarck. Oswald Spengler set
the pace with his *Preussentum und Sozialis-
mus*, which in the fall of 1919 preached a new
nationalistic Prussian socialism (a strange use
for that word) in an essay which culminated
with the words: "We need hardness, we need
a class of socialist master men (*Herrennaturen*)
. . . power, power, and ever more power."[15]

A year before he had published his morpho-
logical study of history, *The Decline of the
West*, which denied the existence of history as
it had been understood by Christianity and
by rationalism. The naturalistic organic theory is driven in his later books to its last ex-
tremes. Culture is for Spengler a natural

growth like a plant. *"Kultur ist ein Gewächs."*[16] "Humanity has no aim, no idea, no plan, any more than the species of butterflies or of orchids has an aim." Man is or perhaps should be a beast of prey, and Spengler goes on: "If I call man a beast of prey, whom do I offend — man or beast? For the great beasts of prey are noble creatures of the most perfect type and without the hypocritical human morality born of weakness."[17] The decisive factor of history is no longer economics or culture as the nineteenth century thought and as the western nations still continue to think, for which Spengler heaps upon them reproach and contempt. The real form of history is war. "Although peace also forms part of it, it is only a continuation of war by other means."[18] War and force are no longer exceptions, incidents in history which have to be avoided or eliminated as far as possible; they are now the central facts of life and history, their meaning and fulfillment.

This cult of force is nothing new or surprising in the twentieth century. It was already there in the second half of the nineteenth century and it has developed since, but only since the World War in the new century has it become a dominant issue. How far all of us have gone on this road we can see from the fact that in 1914, as I said above, the Great War came as a surprise to the majority of the people in every country. Notwithstanding the race of armaments and the long military drills in the barracks of the continental states, the masses were mentally not fully prepared for the War. Today the situation is different. In a similar race of armaments practically everybody thinks war possible, imminent, almost inevitable. Nobody thinks it unimaginable. Few will be surprised when it breaks out, and most of us are happy about peace assurances for even three years. In the nineteenth century men thought themselves secure within a reasonable order. Today they are all afraid, and that is logical, for force begets fear and is itself born of fear.

Force as an ideal can have a meaning only if it is applied so as to arouse fear, the *Schrecklichkeit* of Clausewitz. Fear has not only to be aroused in the weaker or in the attacked; it has also to be aroused in the strong, in the aggressor, who himself has to feel threatened, if not in the actual present experience, at least in his future aspirations which might be thwarted if he does not act now. How necessary fear is for the application of force and the conduct of war Charles James Fox pointed out in his speech on the motion for the suspension of the Habeas Corpus Act in the House of Commons on the thirteenth of May, 1794. The ministers, he said, who had involved the nation in war, "knew that they had no safety but in depriving the people of repose; they knew that if the alarm should be suspended for a moment and if men were allowed time and leisure for the exercise of their understanding, the war, and the principles on which it was undertaken, would be scrutinized and discussed. They dreaded to encounter so hazardous a trial, and all their measures had been directed to keep alive an incessant commotion, so as to suspend every operation of the public intellect. . . . It was to excite the zeal of the people. Zeal was one of those fervent emotions . . . which while it lasted would keep them from examining the object of it. But . . . the zeal which they had aroused was not equal, apparently, to the occasion, and they now strove to awaken a more powerful emotion, that of terror. In short, it was a government of passion, a government in which ministers strove to lull asleep all the sober operations of the mind and to awaken only the fears and terrors of the heart. Reason they dreaded, for reason was their enemy. It was well said by a philosopher of great character that all men dreaded reason who acted against reason."[19]

Has the cult of force produced fear, or is the cult of force an escape from fear? The feeling of fear dominates today the leading expressions of philosophy and theology in Central Europe. The dialectic theology or theology of crisis, the famous manifesto of which appeared characteristically in the year 1918 in Karl Barth's exegesis of the Epistle to the Romans, and the existential philosophy of a man like Martin Heidegger both start, although they arrive at opposite results, from the fear of man who is unprotected and lonely amidst the dangers of life. The revival or rather discovery of the theology of Sören Kierkegaard, which today is to be noticed not only in Germany, where it had already started before the War, but also in France, points in the same direction.[20] Does man need, as Charles James Fox implied, an intoxication to overcome his fear, and does the cult of force, does iron military discipline, does the frenzy of power given to those highest in authority, act as an overcompensation for that weakness which is at the bottom of fear? When subject to fear man feels strong and secure only if he becomes a member of a great army. Thus the ideal of the army, of discipline, of the inequality of rank, becomes a general form into which all manifestations not only of political but also of cultural and economic life are molded.

This holds true of the educational system above all. Under the present regime in Germany this was clear from the outset. In Italy under the leadership of Giovanni Gentile a compromise was first attempted, stressing the intellectual disciplines and scholarship. This compromise has been completely discarded since 1931, when Count de Vecchi became Minister of Education in Italy. He had been one of the original *Quadrumviri*, and he had been praised by Mussolini in 1925 for his unquestioning discipline and subordination in the service of Fascism, or better, of *Il Duce*. As Minister of Education he transformed fundamentally the educational reforms of Gentile and divested them of their intellectual content. The center of gravity was shifted from philosophy in the secondary schools to military education, and the basis of the whole educational system became the three key words of Mussolini — *credere, obbedire, combattere*. An education on this basis is of course foreign to the spirit of scholarship.

That the cult of force must lead to conflicts and catastrophes is self-evident and is not denied by its devotees. On the contrary, the whole content of their teaching is the preparation for the coming conflict. The cult of force is dangerous today because it goes hand in hand, both in its origin and in its practice, with another fundamental issue of our time, the distrust and disregard of reason. A new barbarian has risen and threatens to destroy rational order. Spengler voices his joy over this newcomer: "The age-old barbarism which for centuries lay bound and hidden under the severe discipline of a high culture is again awakening, that warlike healthy joy in one's own strength, which despises the age of rationalistic thought and literature, that unbroken instinct of a strong race which wishes to live otherwise than under the pressure of a mass of books and bookish ideals."[21]

But the new barbarian is different from former barbarians. He comes equipped with the latest devices and instruments of technique. He despises reason, but he accepts and cultivates science and technology and puts them to a new demoniacal use. Without the guidance of reason, without a faith in man and humanity, all our achievements and discoveries become meaningless tools of destruction. It is questionable how far force can be creative and productive in exceptional circumstances, but there seems no doubt that force, veering round in an intellectual vacuum, can only result in the most unbridled reign of terror, which threatens to undermine the foundations of civilization.

THE DETHRONEMENT OF REASON

Of all the faculties of the human mind, it will,
I presume, be admitted that Reason stands at
the summit.
— DARWIN, *The Descent of Man*, I, ii, 46.

CHAPTER II

THE DETHRONEMENT OF REASON

THE philosophy of Descartes who lived in the first half of the seventeenth century is generally considered as the starting point of modern philosophy, as the first clear and well-defined expression of the new intellectual climate which was to become general in the eighteenth and nineteenth centuries. Many preparatory elements of thought were molded by him into a lasting foundation, the rock on which the coming intellectual structure of modern Europe was built. The details of his system are antiquated today. Later philosophers, Locke and Hume, Bayle and Voltaire, Leibnitz, Herder, and Kant, have built upon Descartes's foundations and transformed them beyond anything Descartes could have recognized as his. What has remained as a guiding light is the methodical principles from which he started.

He began by proclaiming doubt as a legitimate attitude of the human mind, the duty and the right of man to scrutinize and analyze every tenet and every opinion until he arrives

at a last self-evident truth. Above the gate-
way to knowledge he inscribed: "*De omnibus
dubitandum*." He accepted no dogma, no
authority. One truth only seemed to him beyond doubt — "*cogito, ergo sum*" ("I think,
therefore I am").

Modern man has grown to intellectual
maturity through this attempt. On its behalf the fight against credulity was waged,
against the acquiescence in current opinions
and traditions, against second- and third-
hand thinking. Descartes's method put upon
man the duty to think for himself and not to
rest until he arrived at a clear and distinct
perception. "*Omne est verum, quod clare et
distincte percipio*." Have the courage to think
for yourselves; fight the inertia which allows
others to think for you; never desist until you
have a clear and distinct perception of what
you think. A new self-confidence was awakened in man, a new dignity given to him. On
the strength of his reason man rose to the position from which he was able to understand
the world.

This new rationalism had far-reaching consequences which Descartes could not foresee
and which he personally would not have
accepted. It made man independent, his own
lawgiver. Reason, the natural light in man,

made superfluous all supernatural and super-
human light. Natural law, law founded upon
human reason, which is the same in all men,
and not law founded upon divine authority,
guided man's steps from philosophical rationalism to political and social rationalism which
found its expression in the American and
French revolutions. In them for the first time
men claimed the right to order society on
rational principles, starting from the self-evident truth that all men are created equal,
that they are endowed with certain unalien-
able rights, and that governments are insti-
tuted to secure these rights and derive their
powers from the consent of the governed.
The application of rationalism to political and
social life created the most far-reaching revolutions in history. An immense new self-
confidence arose in man, a belief in progress
which would be the work of man's labor and
thought, a faith in the perfectibility of man
and of society according to the guidance of
reason.

Modern civilization was prepared in a long
struggle from Descartes to the French Revolution. The occult and dark powers, superstitions and prejudices, seemed routed by
reason. The world seemed *entzaubert*, the
magic taken out of it, the power of the demons

and witch-doctors broken.[22] European mankind had started an apparently unending
march towards truth and towards happiness.

What we call Europe, not as a geographical
but as a spiritual entity, was born in those
years through painful labor. The intellectual
birth pangs of the decisive period have been
admirably analyzed by Paul Hazard in his
treatise on *La Crise de la Conscience Européenne, 1680–1715,* who has given therein the
following definition of Europe: "What is
Europe? A thought which is never satisfied.
Without self-pity, she never ceases her pursuit
of two quests, one towards happiness, the
other, which is even more indispensable to
her and more dear, towards truth. She has
scarcely found an estate which corresponds to
this double requirement when she becomes
aware, when she knows, that as yet she only
holds with an insecure grip something temporary and relative: and she returns to the des-
perate search which is her glory and her
torment."[23]

The faith in man and reason gave Europe
two centuries of unprecedented greatness.
Out of the right and duty of man to think for
himself grew a new toleration, a feeling of
respect for the rights and opinions of one's
fellow man, for his freedom of thought, an

effort to arrive at a mutually satisfactory settlement of disputes and discrepancies by discussion and compromise.

But soon doubts made themselves heard. Is man's reason really the dominating factor in his life? Can he find truth? Is he entitled to happiness and truth?

I think it is going too far to describe the eighteenth century and the French Revolution as a revolt against tradition and history in the name of reason. The Revolution itself had deep historic roots, and the desire of man for a new and better world which finds its expression in the Revolution is, in my opinion, as deeply rooted in the inner man — if not more deeply — as any warlike or "we-group" instinct or any loyalty to a leader. With certain reservations, however, Lord Acton is right in calling romanticism the "revolt of outraged history against the new ideas by calling up the old," a revolt of the traditional interests and sentiments against the new, daring effort of men to create a more rational order.

This romanticism as a political and social philosophy was especially strong in Germany. It found a clear expression in the famous debate between the two leading German jurists of that time. Anton F. J. Thibaut, then professor of law in Heidelberg, published a pamphlet in 1814 about the necessity of the codification of civil law for Germany, where at that time the most dire confusion ruled, each of the many German states having its own law, mostly antiquated and expressing the spirit of past centuries. He was answered by Friedrich Carl von Savigny, then professor of law at the newly founded University of Berlin, the center of the nationalistic teaching of those days, in a pamphlet entitled *Vom Beruf unsrer Zeit für Gesetzgebung und Rechtswissenschaft* ("Of the Vocation of Our Age for Legislation and Jurisprudence"), which became a rallying point of political and legal reaction.[24] Savigny opposed the rational codification of law, for to him law was an organic growth, an emanation of the *Volksgeist*, and courts of law acted not as the exponents of a common reason but as representatives of the *Volksgeist*. It is noteworthy that in the debate between the two scholars Savigny and romanticism remained victorious in Germany. Romanticism glorified the instinct, the unconscious working of the *Volksgeist*, ancient traditions the roots of which are lost in the dim past, the venerability of everything which is hoary, the wisdom of the Middle Ages.

But romanticism in the first half of the

nineteenth century remained a countercurrent, an important countercurrent which
could serve to remind man of the strength of
irrational forces; but the main current belonged indisputably to rationalism. It triumphed with Hegel and the Left wing of his
school in German philosophy, with the early
Victorians in England, with Marx in socialism. The whole nineteenth century, even its
latter half, was dominated by faith in reason
and progress. The immense forward strides
made by science, the new discoveries, the expansion of European domination all over the
earth made possible through the superiority
of European civilization, gave to the European man a feeling of unmeasured pride in his
achievements, in the rationalistic foundations
of his civilization.

In the heyday of Hegel's power only one
philosopher had dared radically to dethrone
reason. For Schopenhauer reason was no
longer the great creative force by which man
became godlike, it was only an instrument of
passing importance which the real master of
the world had created for his practical use.
Will, the dark and blind urge, is the real
essence of the world. This will, which
Schopenhauer defines as the will to live without any definite aim or purpose, used intelli-

gence only to shed some flickering light in the immense darkness of life. Schopenhauer's principal work, *The World as Will and Idea*, which appeared in 1818, remained practically unknown until the beginning of the second half of the last century, and even then, although its fame grew, its pessimism remained an isolated phenomenon of philosophical interest which did not influence many.

It captivated, however, the imagination of two men of genius, Wagner and Nietzsche. Wagner sent Schopenhauer a copy of his Nibelungen Ring in 1854, thanking him for his theory of music; for Schopenhauer had declared music the highest, because the most irrational, form of art, the most naked and unreflected expression of the essence of life, of will. Wagner's work became an exposition of Schopenhauer's philosophy to which he added the ideas of Gobineau's racial theories which had appeared at that time in the great treatise, "On the Inequality of the Human Races."

Nietzsche transformed Schopenhauer's doctrine of the will to live into a doctrine of the will to power. Schopenhauer was deeply pessimistic, as the dark irrational forces implied the complete meaninglessness of life. Nietzsche forced himself by heroic effort into optimism. He saw the tragedy of life, its apparently meaningless cruelty, but he proclaimed it the duty of modern man to be heroic in the face of all the meaningless hardships and to say a jubilant "yes" to the tragedy of life. His *amor fati* was a great appeal to love of life in defiance of everything. He had no faith in the common man, no hope of progress, no confidence in the power of reason. What he looked for was an irrational justification of life as against all reason, "a justification of life, even where it was most terrible, most equivocal, and most false." Nietzsche glorifies life and trusts it — irrational, blind life which creates and destroys endlessly without any rational purpose — for Nietzsche knew that not only was the Christian God dead but also the rational moral values which had been, in his opinion, nothing else than a secularized Christianity. He outlined his program in sharp words. "The principal innovation ... instead of moral values nothing but naturalistic values. Naturalization of morality. In the place of sociology a doctrine of the forms of dominion." The will to power is the only meaning of life, a desire to live, to live doggedly, to wish to live forever, again and again, in eternal recurrence.[25]

Nietzsche had a unique power of psychological diagnosis of men and of his time. He illuminated unsuspected depths of the human character, never reached before. He felt European civilization threatened by disintegration, not an economic disintegration but something which reaches infinitely deeper, a moral and intellectual disintegration, destroying all the accepted standards and leaving men in a complete vacuum. Against this nihilism Nietzsche attempted a revaluation of all values. This deep moralist, like a most delicate seismograph, felt the coming earthquake at a time when all the others continued to live as if their foundations were unshakable rock. Out of despair and fear, out of distrust of the common man and his liberties, he proclaimed the superman. In the midst of the disintegration which he felt coming, he preached hardness, virility, fighting virtues, not it is true for the battlefield of mechanized arms, but for the more difficult and more dangerous decisions in the intellectual realm. To us today his heroic and lonely effort seems only to have increased the nihilism and the chaos, the lack of intellectual orientation and order, in which we live today.

Nietzsche himself had rationalism and Christian morality deep in his blood. Perhaps that was the reason why he felt more strongly than others how near was danger. Only a quarter of a century later the intellectual elite of Europe had become aware of a growing distrust of reason and the glorification of life beyond good and evil. The absolute rationalism of Hegel had been first undermined by our fast-growing knowledge of history, by our widening of the horizons, through the discoveries in archeology, prehistory, and ethnology. The historical method seemed to lead to a relativization of all positions, but the historical method had to give way at the end of the century to a new method which drew its principles and its inspiration from biology. Modern psychology stressed at the same time irrational or pre-rational motives as guiding motives in man's life. The subconscious seemed to play a much larger part in life and history than the nineteenth century had supposed. Man seemed subject to biological forces against which his reason was powerless, of which his reason perhaps was only an accessory and an instrument. Organic and vitalistic theories gained ground in all social sciences. *Bios*, life, triumphed over *ethos* and *logos*. A new interest in romanticism arose at the beginning of the twentieth century. Long-forgotten authors were reëdited and read.

The heart and the soul were praised at the expense of reason and intellect. The irrational forces in men and society seemed not only the true directives, but they seemed also the only creative forces able to lift men up to enthusiasm and great deeds, to liberate them from the dryness and meanness of intellectual life. Out of the unknown dark depths of man where he seemed in intimate contact with nature, earth, and race, out of his instincts, salvation could come.[26]

Glorification of life and distrust of reason led to a new *Verzauberung* of the world, its derationalization, the reappearance and recrudescence of old superstitions, a new triumph of magicians and witch doctors, equipped this time with all the newest devices of technique and mass hypnosis. What had been an esoteric teaching among the intelligentsia before the World War became after the World War a fundamental issue with the younger generation. In the growing complexity of the world, after the unprecedented catastrophe of the World War, the bewilderment of the masses led them to a growing impatience with and distrust of reason. This happened just at the time when it would have been most important to mobilize all our rational forces and all our patient efforts, all our critical faculties for ordering the post-war world so as to avoid even graver catastrophes.

Modern civilization is based upon an active affirmation of life and on the faith that human reason can transform this life to greater justice, to greater freedom, to greater happiness for all. It is a faith in ethical progress, in a deep meaning of history, in culture not as the sum of literature and intellectual and aesthetic refinement but as the application of man's spirit to order the world according to his ideals.

Today civilization in the modern sense seems endangered. The faith in progress guided by reason and ethics is weakened, the faith in the dignity of man as such and therefore in the equality of men is assailed in many quarters. What remains there, where the attack has been successful, is the tremendous urge of life, its representation by powerful individuals and races, a belief in technique, in discipline, in uniform masses in which the individual seems to find a better and safer satisfaction of the urge for life. The objectivity of truth and the quest for it are abandoned for a vitalistic pragmatism. The hope for happiness is belittled; life is tragic and has to be accepted as such. Man has to bear undaunted its tragedy and can find his satisfaction only in struggle and conquest, in self-sacrifice and in the greatness of the group. As life has lost its meaning, as happiness is unattainable, what remains is the expression of man's primitive vitality in fight and action where man threatens man, one people the other people, and where we seem returned to the primitive chaos, *homo homini lupus*, or better, *populus populo lupus*, only that in primitive society wolves had no long-range guns and no poison gas.

In those quarters thinking is being discredited, action praised. Signor Mussolini in his article on "The Political and Social Doctrine of Fascism" points out at the beginning that Fascism in the first years had no doctrine. The leader and his followers did not bother to think. "My own doctrine," says Mussolini, "had always been a doctrine of action." What they hastened to do was to act, and Signor Mussolini goes on: "What was more important and more sacred [than doctrine and thinking] — men died. They knew how to die. Doctrine might be lacking; but there was to take its place something more decisive — Faith." "*Sono un camminatore*," Mussolini proclaims; "I am always on the way, I always go on."[27]

It would probably seem to these activists

old-fashioned to object that it is not so important that men die and that men know how to die, but that it is most important that if men die they die for a good purpose. It is good to be on the road, but the most important thing is to know where the road leads, not to start before the way is mapped out and the destination chosen. But large parts of humanity today seem impatient with thinking, with the hard discipline which thinking requires, tired of the "ifs" and "buts," desiring only to act, to move, to march, especially to march in masses, to feel the comradeship of masses, to overcome the loneliness, the fear which descends upon man in the growing complexity of our situation. The words which are preached in Italy are not the words of thinking, but of action. We hear again and again *conquistare, creare, realizzare, costruire, attuare, immedissimare.*

Discussion and contemplation are not cultivated, reason is ridiculed in present-day Germany. What the youth gets is unthinking enthusiasm. A state of mind of uncritical enthusiasm, of discipline and unquestioning subordination to authority, is characteristic only of war or as a preparation for war. In a world where reason and ethics are disregarded we are back at the *bellum omnium contra omnes*, at the struggle for existence unhampered by what is regarded today by many as sentimental humanitarianism. Might creates right. The objectivity of law is declared a liberal prejudice. Right is what helps in the struggle for power. In a world like that all security has disappeared. The abstract majesty of law is gone. The concrete situation alone and its supposed needs decide. A treaty or an obligation is valued and kept only as long as it is deemed useful. Every certainty is gone: the unforeseen may happen at any moment. Fear grows everywhere, and fear only begets more fear. With all the talk and glorification of courage and courageous living, the essential form of courage which distinguishes man seems to have become extremely rare in our days — the courage to face the fundamental issues, to think for himself, and to understand, as Descartes has said it, that " that is true which can be clearly and distinctly perceived."

Like thinking, language has lost its general validity and clarity. Words have acquired during the last years an ambiguous meaning. Acts which were regarded as disgraceful get today high-sounding names which hide their real nature. One of the most important tricks of the great magicians of today is to add to the confusion of our time by a new terminology. There seems less and less a basis for a common understanding, for a productive conversation between men of different political creeds.

Reason is a powerful bond to unite all mankind: their equality, their common interests are recognized. Today with the stress upon instincts, traditions, and heredity it is the differences between men and between races which emerge, a perpetuation of the past without any hope for a better future.

Even science does not unite any more — the old Republic of Letters is gone. Science tends to become in some countries, as Ernst Kriek called it, "*Wehr, Waffe, und Werkzeug zum völkischpolitischen Aufbau*," arms and tools for the nationalist political upbuilding. Science in some countries no longer pursues knowledge for the sake of truth. It no longer serves the progress of all humanity. It is an instrument for national purposes and it is therefore divided into national sciences according to the different national purposes.[28] Sometimes the national science is even believed to be different in its origin, in its method, and in its results, according to the biological and materialistic forces of blood and soil which are deemed stronger than the spirit.

Does this dethronement of reason mean the end of our civilization, the definite decline of the Occident and its moral and intellectual disintegration, or is it only a crisis in our civilization? We cannot answer this question with any certainty, but we may be helped in our task by a historical retrospect. We are sometimes inclined today to forget what the nineteenth century really meant in human history. The period from the American and French revolutions to the World War is not comparable to any preceding century in the history of mankind as far as it is known to us. It is a period which is *sui generis*, which is distinct from the whole preceding period of man's existence. During those one hundred and fifty years a greater progress was achieved than in all the centuries before. This progress did not express itself solely or mainly in the domain of science and technology. In those fields it is well known that there was a greater difference between 1930 and 1830 than between 1830 and 1530. Neither does the progress express itself mainly in the almost incredible rise of the standard of life, of wealth, of comfort, of health, in the considerable increase of the average length of life, in all classes of society in those countries where modern civilization has prevailed. The essential progress of the last one hundred and fifty years lies, in my opinion, in three other directions — towards the equality of man, towards a more general participation of everybody in the fullness and opportunities of life, and towards a refinement and humanization of our mores. In all these three fields we are very far from the goal, but we have gone further towards it than any preceding period.

A brief survey will show how far we have gone in these three directions. Only one hundred and fifty years ago and even less slavery and serfdom were generally accepted and were the rule in most countries. Everywhere in the European countries a high barrier of legal inequality separated classes and castes. Slavery and serfdom have disappeared today, at least legally, everywhere, and even Fascist Italy proclaimed as one of her aims in Ethiopia the abolition of slavery. At the end of the nineteenth century in practically all civilized countries the legal equality of all men was established, and in the backward countries the fight for civilization included the fight for the equality of all. This has never been known in history before.[29]

Equality was regarded as a natural right, but the opponents of equality could claim that nowhere in nature does equality exist. Rousseau recognized that fully when he said: "It is precisely because the force of circumstances always tends to destroy equality that the force of legislation should always tend to maintain it."[30] Legal equality puts the weak on the same footing as the strong, protects him against the naturally superior, affords him in principle the same opportunities as they enjoy who are more privileged by nature. In the service of the common good each individual had to reach his fullest possible development. The fight for the equality of men, for the abolition of slavery, serfdom, and caste privileges, was one of the greatest triumphs of the spirit of man.[31]

The same is true about the unprecedented effort to throw open the treasures of art and knowledge, the richness and opportunities of life, to the great masses of the people. What had been restricted in all preceding civilizations to a small minority, generally a minority consisting only of males, was now in a great concerted effort made more and more the common property of everybody, men and women of all classes and walks of life. A very important step forward has been made even during the last years by the development of adult education. As the nineteenth century established through long effort the general education of children, the twentieth will establish general adult education. We are yet far from the end of the road, but wherever European civilization penetrated in the nineteenth century it brought with it in principle the new gospel of the right of everybody to education, to happiness, to comfort.

In the refinement and humanization of morals and mores, we have perhaps not surpassed the best of the ancient Stoics, their philosophy of *philanthropia* and *humanitas* (Seneca's *homo homini res sacra*), but what remained with them the cultured refinement of a very small elite had grown in the nineteenth century into a vast reform movement to eradicate in the masses and in all countries as far as possible the cruelty and the apathy which were commonly and generally accepted as natural one hundred and fifty years ago. We have only to think back to what appears to us today as the inhuman treatment of criminals, lunatics, the poor, and the children which existed then even in the most civilized countries to measure the road which we have traveled, thanks to Beccaria and other humanitarians who inculcated in us a new consciousness of social responsibility. One hundred and fifty years ago men were not only condemned to death for trifling offenses, but were put to death by the most calculated torture. Lunatic asylums, prisons, poorhouses, were places of unspeakable horror. Corporal punishment was general. Children were seldom protected in their weakness and immaturity. There is no doubt that in all these respects immense progress was achieved in all the countries of modern civilization during the nineteenth century. It was a long struggle and we are certainly still very far from the ideal: the nineteenth-century movement had its shortcomings, its hypocrisies, its absurdities, but it was a great and serious effort to make life more human and more reasonable. It brought in the countries of modern civilization an increase of liberty, welfare, and happiness as had no century before.[32]

This tremendous progress in such a relatively short time demanded a unique effort on the part of man. The ever-increasing pace of invention and production demanded ever new adjustments. No rest was given to man in his efforts. Industrialism, science, democracy, had brought a permanent unrest into life. No sooner was a stage reached than it was surpassed and left behind.

To this difficulty in the tempo of the development another fundamental difficulty was added, that of its growing extent. Modern civilization as it developed in the nineteenth century did not remain confined to an educated minority or to a definite number of countries. Although it originated with the educated classes of Western Europe, it carried within itself from the beginning a universal message. Based upon the faith in common reason and the equality of man, it appealed to every man and to every people and tried to draw the masses and the most distant countries into its train. The progressive nations and the upper and middle classes tried to monopolize modern civilization and to exploit on its strength the backward nations and the lower classes. But the dynamics of its ideas could not be stopped. They had from their origin a universal scope and message. They penetrated to the masses and to backward peoples: the monopoly could not exist in the face of the immanent dynamic and universal character of rational civilization. The dynamic character of ideas was intensified by the dynamics of industrialism, with its permanent increase of production, its demand for new markets and for new raw materials. Thus modern civilization had the task of carrying growing masses in all countries with it, to awaken them from their apathy, to train them for their participation in a richer and fuller life. Those masses had never been integrated before into a living civilization. They had lived under the dead weight of tradition. The problem before civilization today is not to lament "the revolt of the masses," but to try to integrate them into a civilization which for the first time is not an aristocratic civilization; a task of the greatest difficulty as it demands the continuous readjustment and enlargement of civilization.

It is possible to argue that this tremendous effort was too much for men, that we have arrived, at least temporarily, at the end of our strength, that we are fatigued and exhausted. The dark magic forces of the world against which during more than a century the fight was waged do reassert themselves. More and more we seem to capitulate before them. Is rational civilization in temporary retreat or has mankind in an effort of unparalleled intensity reached the limit of its power of rational ordering? Are we not too impatient in view of the brevity of the time involved? No historian can answer these questions. A historian can analyze the past, can try to interpret it and show how it came about. Should he try to construct the future out of the past, then he is easily liable to choose among the bricks of the past for the new edifice those for which he has a preference and to create a new age according to his desires. He cannot say more than what Friedrich Meinecke, the greatest living German historian before the advent of the Nazi regime, has said in comparing our time with that of the generation of Ranke and the first half of the nineteenth century: *"Die geschichtliche Welt liegt dunkler und in dem Charakter ihres ferneren Verlaufs ungewisser und gefährlicher vor uns, als* [Ranke . . .] *sie sah. Denn ihre Natur- und Nachtseite hat sich für unser Denken und unsere Erfahrung als mächtiger herausgestellt. Aber der Geist darf nicht ablassen, sich gegen sie zu behaupten."* ("The historical world stretches before us darker, more uncertain, and more threatening than our fathers thought, as regards the nature of its further course. For the full strength of the instinctive and dark powers of history has revealed itself to our thinking and our experience. But human intelligence must not cease to maintain itself against them.")

With the dethronement of reason, the cult of force assumes even more threatening dimensions,[33] and as any rational control of the

employment of force disappears, force becomes an end in itself, at the same time an instrument and a stimulant of the instinct for
power and domination. This happens just at
the time when we need as never before all our
rational forces to solve the great problem of
reordering human society under the fast-
changing circumstances brought about by
the spread of civilization and the new technology. The problem was in the nineteenth
century a European problem, confined to the
white race. In the twentieth century, as
never before, it has become a universal problem. The spread of modern civilization to the
other races — the work of the movement
which we generally call imperialism — ren-
ders the situation in which we live even more
complex, the dangers even greater, the decisions we take even more portentous. Many
generations in history have been convinced
that they were passing through epochs of
unique importance, but there are reasons to
believe that we have arrived at a turning
point as no other generation before us —
again to use the word, a totalitarian turning
point — and that a responsibility greater than
any before rests with our generation. Many,
however, seem decided to avoid shouldering

the responsibility. They take refuge in the cult of force and in the intoxication of irrationalism. But this escape can only end in increasing the confusion and in precipitating the catastrophe.

Dass dasjenige, was bisher noch nicht gelungen
ist, darum auch nie gelingen werde, berechtigt
nicht einmal, eine pragmatische oder tech-
nische Absicht (wie z.B. die der Luftfahrten
mit aerostatischen Ballen) aufzugeben; noch
weniger aber eine moralische, welche, wenn
ihre Bewirkung nur nicht demonstrativ un-
möglich ist, Pflicht wird. Überdem lassen sich
manche Beweise geben, dass das menschliche
Geschlecht im ganzen wirklich in unserm
Zeitalter in Vergleichung mit allen vorigen
ansehnlich selbst zum moralisch Besseren
fortgerückt sei (kurzdauernde Hemmungen
können dagegen nichts beweisen); und dass das
Geschrei von der unaufhaltsam zunehmenden
Verunartung desselben gerade daher kommt,
dass, wenn es auf einer höheren Stufe der
Moralität steht, . . . sein Urteil über das, was
man ist, in Vergleichung mit dem, was man
sein sollte, . . . desto strenger wird, je mehr
Stufen der Sittlichkeit wir . . . schon erstiegen
haben. — KANT, *Über den Gemeinspruch: Das
mag in der Theorie richtig sein, taugt aber nicht
für die Praxis.*

CHAPTER III

THE CRISIS OF IMPERIALISM

THE word "imperialism" covers many meanings.[34] For our purposes we wish to understand by imperialism that movement of expansion which in the nineteenth century, especially in the second half, and in the twentieth century, carried the influence of the European race into those continents which were mainly inhabited by non-European races, and which in varying degree established a political and economic control of Europe over those countries. This imperialism, like most movements in history, was complex in its origin and even more complex in its results.

We may distinguish two main urges in imperialism, an economic and a psychological. Industrialism with its increasing productivity demanded more and more markets and raw materials. Capitalism with its growth looked for new possibilities of investment. The continents of Asia and Africa had to be opened up to the flow of modern economic life. It has been said lately that colonial imperialism was unproductive for the mother countries from an economic point of view. This may be true

in some respects, but imperialism has undoubtedly been economically advantageous at
least to small and influential groups in the
mother countries. Certainly without the economic opening up of Asia and Africa, whether
in colonial or in other forms, modern industrial life could never have developed as it did
and the working masses in the highly industrialized countries could never have reached
that standard of life which was characteristic
of the skilled workers in the later industrial
development.

Besides the economic urge, psychological
motives played a great role in imperialism —
the lust for adventure and for power, the
added prestige and glory which seemed to
accrue from a vast colonial empire not only to
the governing classes but even to the masses
of the colonizing nations, the new sentiment
of pride and superiority which animated even
the lowest members of the white races in
their dealings with the "backward" races.

Whatever the origins and original motives
of imperialism, its effects went far beyond any
of the intentions of the imperialists. In history we find again and again that the effects
of our action reach far beyond the original
motives, that they produce new chains of motivations and effects, and that finally the ulti-

mate effect may turn out to be entirely different from and even opposed to the original
intentions.

Imperialism opened up the closed continents
in the interests of the white race, its economic
and political power. As the child of a century
in which the Christian motivation of missionaries — often itself in a rationalized and
socially secularized form — combined with
the humanitarian motivation of rationalism
and democracy, imperialism brought with it
not only European merchandise and European methods of administration and exploitation, but also the gospel of the new European civilization, the new message of the
liberty of man, of the equality before the
law, of the quest for happiness. Even against
the will of the imperialist this new message
seeped through. It came through the schools,
few though they were, from the rare books
and newspapers, from the daily contact,
from the example set by the few merchants,
officers, and missionaries. In the long run an
economic exploitation of the colonial or semi-
colonial countries was impossible without the
modernization and mechanization of at least
part of their economic life and means of communication. This process demanded, at least
to a certain degree, the initiation of the na-

tives into modern civilization. Not only for humanitarian reasons had the local diseases to be fought and an elementary understanding of science and mechanics to be transmitted.

Except in the case of Japan the masses of the people in Asia and Africa resisted in the nineteenth century as far as possible the influence of the new civilization. They underwent it passively, they accepted it with resignation, they were not stirred by it, and they were not awakened out of their lethargy into the spirit of activism which characterized the new civilization.

This attitude was entirely changed in the twentieth century. The situation had been altered then in two respects. At the time of the outbreak of the World War the whole earth was mapped out and practically partitioned, whereas even in the middle of the nineteenth century the greatest part of the African continent was still unknown to us and the deserts and plateaus of the interior of Asia had hardly been explored. China and Japan had just been opened. Sixty years later there was hardly a spot not yet penetrated by the white man.

Even in the last years before the World War the means of communication in Asia and Africa were still the ancient ones in use since time immemorial. With the exception of a very few railways, men and goods depended for transportation upon native bearers, camels, or mules. Since the War, however, the motor car and the airplane have achieved a revolution of an unforeseen scope. The ancient notions of time and space have been completely overturned. Villages have been wrenched from their seclusion. Modern civilization has taken the native masses by storm, forced them, even against their will, to adjust to the new ways, to awaken from their traditional lethargy.

In an astonishingly short time Asia has been completely changed, and Africa may now follow. In the thirty years between 1905 and today old and venerable oriental theocracies and monarchies have given way to secularized republics where the people are educated to an active participation in the national life. We have been accustomed during these last years to speak of the revolt of the East, of the effort to throw off the yoke of western domination, to win back independence. But it is a changed independence: it is not a return to the past. The past is gone irrevocably for the East as it is for Europe. No romantic longing of Gandhi or of some Confucianists in China can bring it back.

This revolt of the East is a very recent phenomenon. It started only about 1905 when Japan defeated Russia; when the age-old monarchies in Turkey, Persia, and China were shattered to their foundations; when the two great imperial pro-consuls of Great Britain in the East — Lord Curzon and Lord Cromer — left their imperial wards as a new day dawned in India and Egypt. Since then we have witnessed the astonishing transformation of all the oriental countries, a movement which has been aptly described as decolonization, an apparent reversal of the tide of the nineteenth century.

This movement is much more than political, than an attempt to cast off foreign control. The brevity of time and the rapidity of the transformation do not always allow the observer to gauge the depths of the transformation which is going on with increasing momentum and tends completely to recast the intellectual, social, and economic life of those countries, although the old forms and appearances still survive in many localities on the surface. This transformation is no longer confined as it was before the World War to the intelligentsia, to a small upper class, but since the World War it has spread to the masses. It is not the coming of the machine, of the motor car, of the radio, of the movie house, of electricity, which is characteristic of this new age. These are only outward signs. The transformation expresses itself in a changed world outlook and intellectual attitude, in the alteration of the traditional patterns of life and behavior, in a new set of wants and demands.

We may try to define this changing outlook by three of its components — rationalism, individualization, and activization. Of course these three elements are closely interlinked, are in themselves of utmost complexity, are found in the most different stages of development, at every step still intermixed with and even dominated by survivals of the older world outlook. There are very great differences from country to country, according to their general situation, past and present. There are great differences from social class to social class, from locality to locality, from individual to individual, but nevertheless the general trend is unmistakable.

Rationalism has come in the East to replace the old traditional outlook in which the world was dominated by religious and magical forces. Rationalism makes itself felt in the social relations where individualism is breaking down more and more the traditional ties of family, clan, and caste, and in economic life where the transition from a barter to a monetary economy and the penetration of modern industrialization force upon the producer and consumer a new attitude. The old easy-going way of life, the methods of work transmitted from generation to generation since time immemorial, the submissive acceptance of the will of despots — of the great despot in the far-off city and of the petty despots nearer by — and of the caprices of nature as inescapable fate — all that which appeared to many only a generation ago as the unchangeable East, is giving way to a new sense of activism, of a conscious will on the part of the masses to change the existing circumstances. They learn that they are entitled to a better life, to more liberty, to the pursuit of happiness. They learn that they are able by organization and coöperation, by revolts, strikes, and demonstrations, to realize some of their new demands and new wants. A new, great eagerness is there for learning, for going to school, for reading. In Asia as well as in distant villages in Africa the position of women is changing rapidly. They have begun to participate not only in the life of their community but beyond that in the life of their nation, in its political aspirations, in its intellectual renaissance. As in all similar circumstances, youth movements have been the foremost exponents of the new ways of life.

All this is only in its initial stage, but it goes on astonishingly fast wherever foreign influences do not try to hamper it. Colonial administrators and their supporters at home like to believe that the nature of the Asiatic or African man is fundamentally different from their own, that there is no possible ground for common attitudes and aspirations, that the Oriental does not want improvement and is happy in his traditional ways. The old ways are surrounded with a halo of romanticism and sanctity, and the distant admirer of the past easily overlooks the corruption and cruel exploitation, the squalor and degeneration, the drabness and utter helplessness, of the traditional life of the masses in the East.

There is no fundamental difference between Orient and Occident. In the times of the Crusades life in Europe was not so very different from life in the Orient. Since then Europe has entered the age of modern civilization in the last two or three centuries, a rational civilization based upon science and a recognition of social obligation, upon the dignity and liberty of the individual and his right to share in

the richness and fullness of life, upon an un-
ceasing fight against utter economic destitu-
tion and misery, against ignorance and back-
wardness. The Orient now enters into this
modern civilization. It has been the half-
involuntary mission of imperialism to have
brought dynamic modern civilization to the
other continents and to have started the mo-
mentous transformation which in the twentieth century has entirely changed the aspect
of humanity. It tends more and more to put
all the peoples of the earth, those who were
progressive in the nineteenth century and
those who were backward then, on an equal
footing, to make them participate in modern
civilization, which has become a universal
civilization in the twentieth century.

This acculturation of the oriental peoples
does not mean of course that the Oriental
will become a European. Every people has its
own character formed by the conditions of its
life and by the traditions of its history. In
Europe in this stage of modern civilization
the different peoples not only retain their
national characteristics, but their national
consciousness has deepened. As far as the
masses are concerned, it has only awakened
since the French Revolution. We find a
similar development in the Orient today. The

awakening of the masses leads them to a new consciousness of nationalism.

With all the differences between people and people, a common mankind is growing up today, not with a common purpose or common organization, not yet with any consciousness of its community, but, whether it is realized or not, with common social, economic, and intellectual problems, anxieties, and hopes. This community of mankind is achieved today for the first time in history. Up to the twentieth century mankind had always lived divided into different civilizations and continents between which there was practically no intercourse and no community of fate. Time and space separated mankind. Some peoples went through the Renaissance and the rationalism of the eighteenth century while other peoples were living in the stone age or continuing a civilization based upon the teachings of the sixth century B.C. Those peoples lived only in a very literal sense at the same time. In no other way were they contemporary. There was no means of an understanding between them. Space separated them as much as time. In the early nineteenth century large parts of the earth were still unknown to us. The difficulty of transportation and travel practically closed most of them to us. Today for the first time the whole earth is known to us and all peoples live in a contemporary world, being able to communicate, not only on account of the new technique of communication but because they have studied and learned for the first time the same things and are faced by the same facts of a changing economic, social, and intellectual order. Therefore the crisis in which we live today can be rightly called a totalitarian crisis.

One aspect of this crisis is the crisis of imperialism. The revolt of the East does not spring from the natural motive which has been there in preceding centuries — to cast off foreign rule, to return to an undisturbed life, and to eliminate all the foreign influences. It is something new in that the Orient has learned that it can resist European aggression only when it adopts modern civilization and when it entirely transforms its own ways of life. It is first in self-defense against the political and economic domination of the white race that the non-white races adopt white civilization. What may have been in the first instance a movement of defense, forced upon the non-white races by their desire for self-preservation — and they have known very well since the end of the nine-

teenth century that the only way towards
self-preservation in the modern world was the
adoption of modern civilization — became
after the World War a ready and active acceptance of modern civilization, of its intellectual virility, of its higher standards of life,
of its greater promises for the mind and for
the body.

Whereas before the World War the main
interests of the movement towards independence in the East were political and cultural,
in the last years they have become economic.
A higher standard of material and cultural
life for the masses can be achieved only with
the thorough betterment of economic conditions. Cultural life certainly does not develop
in direct proportion to economic prosperity.
It may be that too great prosperity stultifies
and degrades cultural life, but there is no
doubt that extreme poverty and misery do
not allow any cultural life and that the most
vital necessities of a decent standard of living
must be secured before the masses can participate in cultural life. This presupposes
for the economically backward countries a
complete recasting of their economic life.
Until now they have been economically ex-
ploited and hampered in their development
by the progressive countries which had used

the backward countries as markets for their
own industrial products, as fields for the investment of their own capital, and as sources
of raw material for their industries.

Now those backward countries have started
to make themselves independent economically, to build their own industries, to accu-
mulate capital for home investment, to protect native industries and native labor against
foreign competition, to modernize and diver-
sify agriculture, and to train their people in
modern methods, in technical and managerial
skill, and in the spirit of enterprise. Since
those countries were drained in the nineteenth century of their gold and silver, and
since the extreme poverty of the people
permits only a very slow accumulation of capital, the national states in the Orient themselves have taken up the task of economic
modernization by a system of state capitalism
which at the same time allows for the training
of the masses and the leaders for the new
tasks. The adoption of modern civilization
leads not only to a political but also to an
economic nationalism.

This of course is again not different from
what is happening in Europe or America, but
it creates a paradoxical situation: while imperialism has introduced modern civilization

to the backward countries, the adoption of
modern civilization by those countries turns
politically and economically against the imperialist countries. The growing prosperity
of the highly industrialized progressive countries in the second half of the nineteenth century was based upon the exploitation of the
backward countries, of Russia, Asia, Africa,
and Latin America. An equilibrium seemed
established which was responsible for the
economic well-being of Europe and North
America in the later nineteenth century. The
countries of the world were divided into two
groups, of which one provided the industrial
manufacture and capital, the other raw materials and cheap labor. This arrangement
worked very well, at least as far as the European and North American nations were concerned, which under this system could build
up their comparatively high standard of life.
It was accepted in the East in the nineteenth
century. It does not meet acceptance today.
This necessarily reacts upon the economic life
and, in the long run, upon the political status
of the western countries. The economic equilibrium of the nineteenth century is upset,
the new unbalance is partly responsible for
the economic crisis which today grips the
highly industrialized countries.[35]

With these changes, imperialism loses the historic justification it had in the nineteenth century. At that time there was a great cultural difference between the western countries and the East. This differential allowed the flow of cultural energies from the more progressive to the backward level. Now, thanks to the involuntary service of imperialism, the levels are becoming more and more equalized. The backward countries are themselves trying to catch up with the progressive. Imperialism has unwillingly rendered a service of historic importance to an unprecedented area. By rendering this service it has destroyed its own basis.

Imperialism has lost another justification. Hume says in his essay "Of the First Principles of Government": "It is . . . on opinion only that government is founded, and this maxim extends to the most despotic and most military governments as well as to the most free and the most popular." [36] In the nineteenth century foreign dominion in backward countries, more so even in the economic than in the political field, was at least passively accepted. The close connection between political and economic control was not understood. The only classes with an articulate opinion welcomed the benefits brought by foreign control and participated in them. This situation has been changed in the twentieth century, when in the backward countries the active and conscious opposition of public opinion to foreign domination has grown to an astonishing degree. Imperialism cannot count any longer on passive acceptance by the masses, and even the number of members of the ruling classes who benefited by coöperation with imperialism is dwindling rapidly.

The crisis of imperialism has also its geographical aspect. In the nineteenth century imperialism offered an outlet for the overflowing energies of the white race. The earth then seemed wide, full of adventure and possibilities of discovery. It was an age of great discoverers and empire builders, courageous men who broke new paths through the wilderness. Romantic glamour combined with rich rewards for the daring mind. There seemed space enough for everybody's expansion. This has changed completely in the twentieth century. We are living on a shrinking earth. Cities which seemed names taken out of legends and fairy tales, like Baghdad or Timbuctoo, can now be reached in a few hours by airplane, and in the jungles of Central Africa the traveller finds hotels with all modern con-

veniences. The world which seemed so vast
a few decades ago is mapped out and partitioned today. There is no room left for the
expansion of warlike races except at the price
of long and heavy conflict.

Again this happens just at a moment when
the cult of force is preached in many quarters,
and expansion and imperialism are glorified.
On a shrinking earth man should concentrate
all his rational forces upon the adjustment of
his social and political life to the new conditions. Instead, we hear reason and reason-
ableness decried and the old battle cries of
fierce imperialism and conflict of races raised
again.

It is interesting to note that at a time when
there are widespread doubts in the western
world about modern civilization and its
foundations, modern civilization has proved
its vitality by spreading over wider areas
than those covered by any civilization before and has revitalized practically the whole
of humanity. In the foreground of the
European scene we see certain leaders franti-
cally agitating and proclaiming at the tops
of their voices — which with the help of
the radio and a highly developed technique
of propaganda are reverberating throughout
the Continent — that modern rational civi-

lization, that progress and the liberty of
the individual, are dead. They hide from
us sometimes another spectacle of our time,
which is less noisy but which is taking place
on an infinitely greater and darker stage. Today everywhere, in China, in India, in the
Soviet Union, in Egypt, in Mexico, masses of
what could be called "sub-human beings" in
our age of "supermen" are awakening out of
their centuries-old lethargy, and the eternal
dumb suffering serfs are breaking through to
a new life, to individuality and personality.
They demand for the first time liberation from
the dead weight of tradition, equality, and
democracy.

A prominent leader of the younger Indian
generation, Subhas C. Bose, has pointed out
in a polemic against Gandhi that "for a
people so prone to mysticism and supernatu-
ralism, the only hope [not only of political]
salvation lies in the growth of a sane rationalism and in the modernization of the material
aspect of life," and that the future of India
lies with the party that will break the isolation that has been India's curse and bring
her into the comity of nations, firm in the
belief that the fate of India is indissolubly
linked with the fate of humanity. The great
leader of the younger generation in India,

whose *Autobiography* is one of the most important and most readable manifestations of the new spirit in the East, Jawaharlal Nehru, goes even farther in his insistence on linking up the fate of the awakening masses of the backward peoples with the rational progress of humanity.[37]

Does this awakening of the backward masses threaten the supremacy of the white race? Oswald Spengler in Germany and Signor Mussolini in Italy have proclaimed the necessity of a united fight of the whole white race in order to maintain its world dominion and to hold the supremacy acquired in the nineteenth century. Some people like to depict the coming struggle of races as the great issue of the twentieth century. Many of the good Pan-Europeans are not so much concerned about Pan-Europe in the interests of universal peace, humanity, and justice as in the preparation for the coming struggle for supremacy of the white race. The cult of force today takes its most extraordinary form in this desire to perpetuate imperialism and the supremacy of the white race.

It seems to me an idle and a dangerous dream. There is no united front of the white race as there is no united front of the non-white races. With the lessening and finally

the overthrow of imperialism in a growing
number of countries, the only bond which
keeps the non-white races together, their
opposition to imperialism, will disappear.
Already Japan is among the imperialistic
countries, and the Union of Socialist Soviet
Republics, which consists today of eight oriental and three occidental sister republics,
where the formerly backward races enjoy
complete equality with the white races, can
hardly be counted as a member of a united
white front to maintain the domination of the
white race. Any attempt to simplify the issue
into a question of whether the white race can
hold and defend the dominating position it
enjoyed in the nineteenth century conjures
up the danger of a coming racial struggle of
unprecedented dimensions, the fear of which
will necessarily strengthen everywhere the
illiberal and bellicose forces which will plunge
humanity into a real Armageddon.[38]

There is no doubt that the process of decolonization, the new defensive economic
nationalism which is now being developed in
the Orient and in Latin America, will put a
heavy strain upon the economic system of the
countries which formerly held the monopoly
of modern industrialism. They will have to
readjust themselves to the new conditions,

and readjustment is always a painful process. Even if the backward countries succeed in a rapid industrialization, they will nevertheless depend for a long time to come on the countries with an older industrial civilization for all products which demand a special skill and a highly developed technique. As the formerly backward countries have to readjust their social order, so will the progressive have to do. With the backward countries it is today above all a problem of increased production; with the progressive countries it will be above all a problem of a better distribution of the produced goods.

The difficulty of the task and the power of the vested interests may try to divert the attention from this task to some expansionist adventure. These adventures can bring no solution. They may postpone the ultimate readjustment, but they will undoubtedly render it more difficult and more painful in the long run. Alexander may have been able to conquer the world in his day by untying the Gordian Knot with a stroke of his sword. In the complex world of today there is no similar shortcut through force possible.

We often hear it said that the numbers of the non-white races are growing in such a proportion that they will in a short time annihilate the white race by sheer numbers. An examination of the figures does not bear out this contention. Most of the figures which we can find for the non-European continents or for non-recent times are only estimates, but the *Encyclopedia of the Social Sciences* gives the estimate considered most reliable in its article on "Population," and I have used it in drawing up the following tables.

Continents Predominantly White

	1650	1800	1900	1930
		(Figures in millions)		
Europe	100	187	401	505
North America	7	15.4	106	168.75
South America	6	9.2	38	82.75
Australia	2	2	6	9.88

Continents Predominantly Non-White

	1650	1800	1900	1930
Asia	250	522	859	992.5
Africa	100	100	141	142.4

We see from these figures that the population of Africa has increased by only about a half in the last three hundred years, Asia about four times; whereas Europe has increased its population five times, not counting all the millions which the European races sent to make the two Americas predominantly white continents. This relatively much larger increase of the white continents even holds good for recent times. In the years from 1900 to 1930 the annual increase per thousand population amounted to an average total of 6.8 all over the world. Both Asia and Africa remained below the average, Asia with 4.8 and Africa with 0.3. On the other hand the increase in Europe averaged 7.8, and the increase of the three other largely white continents was even greater, in North America 15.6, in South America 26.3, and in Australia 16.8. Although these three continents contain considerable minorities of non-white population, nevertheless this increase is largely, perhaps almost entirely, due to the immigration of white population.

The figures quoted above show us that although the non-white races can claim a majority on the surface of the earth, with about 1150 millions as against 750 millions of whites, nevertheless there is no proof for the assertion that the non-white races have until now grown faster than the white. About the tendencies of the future the historian can only say that there are so many unknown factors involved, economic, social, and psychological, that any forecast of the future development would seem arbitrary and would probably express more the personal wishes, hopes, and fears of the author than the real future trends.

What we know definitely is the fact that we are faced today for the first time in history by a situation in which we have to take the whole of humanity into account and in which we have to try to arrive at solutions which embrace not one continent and not one race but all continents and all races equally. In the last one hundred years the population of the earth has grown from about 850 millions who lived in several almost water-tight compartments without economic, cultural, or political contact or with very little of it, to 1900 millions thrown together on a shrinking earth and rubbing shoulders in every field of human activity. At the same time our productive powers have kept pace with the growth of population. Inventions and science have created powers of benevolence and of destruction which seem to realize some of the most extravagant dreams of only a century ago.

The voice of the radio penetrates into the jungles of Africa. The peasant in Turkey or India sees before him on the screen of the movie house in the nearest town which he visits, thanks to the new bus communications, the pictures produced in Hollywood.

The student in Nanking reads the same books
as the student in London. These changes
which came upon us in almost breathless
succession are of course known to us, but they
are only rarely visualized by us in their whole
context and consequences. They have not
yet sunk into our consciousness. It cannot
be otherwise. Never yet has mankind lived
through a period of similar intensity in every
manifestation of social life, never were the
changes so fast and far-reaching, never the
situation so complicated by the complete
interlinkedness and interconnection of the
acts and thoughts of all countries and all
races.

In my opinion the totalitarian crisis in
which mankind today finds itself, a crisis of
unprecedented dimensions and intensity, at
the same time social, intellectual, economic,
and political, is caused by the discrepancy
between the quickly changing reality around
us and the notions, ideas, and sentiments by
which all of us are still dominated. Our conscious, and even more our subconscious, life is
still under the influence of motives and emotions which correspond to a reality which belongs to the past. We are, in our nationalism,
children of the nineteenth century, whereas
the twentieth century drives towards a super-

national order. We are expansionists at a time when there is no room left in which to expand. We speak of backward races and of the inequality of races at a time when even the most backward ones start to take the road towards modern civilization and the more progressive among them try to keep abreast of it. At a time when around us for the first time in history a world community grows up based on a common modern civilization and upon economic interdependence, we take our refuge in provincial-mindedness. In a world changing as never before some try to conjure up again archaic man as he roamed the forests of Germany in the time of Tacitus, or the ghost of the Roman Empire which has, as we know, died long ago in the downfall of a great civilization.

With this discrepancy between reality and our inner life, no end of the crisis is visible. On the contrary, out of the discrepancy we prolong the crisis. We are far from acknowledging the rise of a common humanity. Some tendencies in our time drive us towards more nationalism, towards a sharper accentuation of the differences between the groups. Many of us look more towards the past than towards the future, and some of us even to a very distant past. Our capitalists undermine capitalism which is based upon the free exchange of goods, of men, of capital, by putting up high barriers against commodities, against immigrants, against the flow of credit. The nationalistic self-sufficiency policy must lead to a disintegration of international economic life. In a nationalistic world, dominated by fear of the neighbor and his intentions, any efficient use of the resources of land and raw material in a rational way is impossible, in the same way as a rational handling of the population problem is out of the question. The very much needed general leveling of the standard of life, not only of those relatively very well off countries in Europe which are generally spoken of as the "have-nots" and which are powerful and aggressive enough to have their claims listened to, but even more of those countries in which the masses live in really abject poverty, should have a claim to the consideration of humanitarians.

The crisis of imperialism has helped us to throw some light upon the crisis in which we find ourselves today. The conflict of imperialisms drove nations into the World War. The World War accelerated and increased some of the issues which were already there at the end of the nineteenth century and which were largely responsible for the genesis of the

World War. Today they have become the fundamental issues of our time, threatening us with new wars and new conflicts, more terrible and more widespread than was the World War, which in history may be known later as the First World War.

During the World War some men conceived the idea that to avoid future conflicts international coöperation must be strengthened, that the influence of nationalism must be lessened by a decrease of the sentiments of fear and insecurity which drive the nations to arms, and that the economic welfare and the rise of the standard of living of the lower classes must become an international concern. This conception did not remain entirely sterile. Woodrow Wilson took the first steps towards its realization. The League of Nations and the International Labor Office were created, a meeting place for the first time in history of the representatives of all the nations, of employers and employees, to discuss political, economic, and cultural problems of humanity.

But the realization of international coöperation was obstructed from the beginning by the defection of the United States [39] and by the non-inclusive character of the League, which left out not only the defeated nations of the World War but all the dependent peoples and colonies. In the League of Nations and in the International Labor Office for the first time machinery was set up for world coöperation. It seemed as if some political thinkers and statesmen at least had realized the new fact of the interdependence of humanity. Soon, however, it became clear that no nation yet was ripe for the new idea. The discrepancy between the new reality, visualized as yet only by a very few, and the sentiments and notions which still dominated and dominate the overwhelming majority everywhere, was too great. The machinery did not correspond to any new spirit; it was dominated and used by the old spirit. It seems ridiculous to say that the ideal of international coöperation has failed. It has never been tried. There was in no people the earnest will to try it.[40] The ideal had no influence upon the fundamental issues of our time. They have, in a sense, developed contrary to world coöperation and to any rational reordering of humanity.

The crisis of imperialism may force us in some perhaps not-too-distant future to take stock of the reality around us and to recognize the new world-wide situation. International coöperation, an international order, seem today to many a wild and ridiculous idea, but in history things have frequently come to be accepted which seemed utterly impracticable not long before. As an outstanding progressive liberal of his time, Charles James Fox, as late as 1794, at the end of the fifth year of the French Revolution, regarded universal suffrage as an impossible Utopia. "He had," he told the House of Commons, "constantly and uniformly considered universal suffrage as a wild and ridiculous idea. When his noble relation, the Duke of Richmond, had one day taken pains to explain his ideas on this subject, a learned and ingenious friend of his said to him, with as much truth as wit, 'My Lord, I think the best part of your Grace's plan is its utter impracticability.'"[41] Today we find much less truth and wit in the learned friend's remarks than did his contemporaries.[42]

More to the point was Lord Macaulay, who wrote in January, 1830, in the *Edinburgh Review*, towards the end of his essay on Southey's *Colloquies on Society* (an essay which is still worth while reading, perhaps more today than ever): "If we were to prophesy that in the year 1930 a population of fifty million, better fed, clad, and lodged than the English of our time, will cover these islands, that Sussex and Huntingdonshire will be wealthier than the wealthiest parts of the West Riding of Yorkshire now are . . . that machines constructed on principles yet undiscovered will be in every house, that there will be no highways but railways, no travel but by steam, that our debt, vast as it seems to us, will appear to our great-grandchildren a trifling incumbrance, which might easily be paid off in a year or two, many people would think us insane." History has proven that Macaulay was not insane in uttering this wild and ridiculous prophecy, composed of details of apparently utter impracticability. He was mistaken in only one point. Reality has surpassed even his seemingly insane imagination. We travel again on highways because even the fantastic railways of his day have been surpassed. Macaulay wrote this passage in 1830, a year, as it then seemed to Europe, of crisis and change. Historians are no prophets, but they should view events with a truer perspective than their contemporaries. "To almost all men the state of things under which they have been used to live seems to be the necessary state of things," Macaulay says in the same essay.[43] To the historian the fallacy of this attitude is obvious. There are always new ways and developments opening up in history, and the necessity[44] of avoiding otherwise inescapable catastrophes, and sometimes the guidance of wise statesmanship, force peoples to tread new roads, previously undiscovered or believed impassable.

NOTES

NOTES

1. This comparative peace granted to Europe during the nineteenth century was not given to Asia or Africa. Both continents witnessed tremendous changes — Asia the penetration of European trade and domination, Africa the last recrudescence of the slave trade which confounded, upset, and destroyed the social and moral foundations of Negro life; and scarcely was slave hunting dying out when the equally disruptive capitalistic exploitation of the natives set in. Even in Asia and Africa, however, the changes of the nineteenth century led to far-reaching social and intellectual transformations only after the World War.

2. The Holy Alliance was not an effort at the restoration of the pre-revolutionary international order. Politically and in its underlying philosophy reactionary, it was nevertheless from the point of view of international law and order progressive. It continued, in a changed form, the cosmopolitan tendencies of the French Revolution and of Napoleon, the wish to give Europe a new international organization which would not be based upon dynastic or state interests, but upon principles. Cf. B. Mirkine-Guetzévitch, "L'Influence de la Révolution Française sur le Developpement du Droit International dans l'Europe Orientale," Académie du Droit International, *Recueil des*

Cours, XXII (Paris, 1929), 447 ff. The two basic
ideas of the Holy Alliance, the application of
ethical principles to political life and the unity of
all nations under a higher sovereignty, were undoubtedly progressive and will have to be recon-
sidered by the twentieth century, but they were
based on thoughts of a past age, a confused and reactionary mysticism. This discrepancy between
the changing reality around the Holy Alliance and
the sentiment and interests of a past age on which
the Alliance was built prevented the Holy Alliance
from becoming more than pious words and hopes.
It lacked the sense for the growing new reality and
it lacked sincerity. Under changed circumstances,
with the progress of the nineteenth century in between, the League of Nations took up some of the
basic ideas of the Holy Alliance. The essential
weaknesses of the League of Nations make us
better understand the essential weaknesses of the
Holy Alliance.

3. The highly praised achievements of Bismarck appear to many today in a different light.
A leading English historian, G. P. Gooch, who before and after the World War has shown in his
books the warmest sympathy for and understanding of German mentality and aspirations, arrives
finally at the following judgment: "Vast and
splendid as was his [Bismarck's] intellect, the
vision of a new international order resting on a
partnership of contented self-governing national
units was beyond his ken. The main task of the

twentieth century as it emerges from the shattering ordeal of the war, is the organization of a shrinking world. To the shaping of the human spirit for that supreme adventure, Bismarck contributed nothing either by example or precept. He was content to work for his country alone and was satisfied with its rapturous applause." (*Studies in Modern History*, London: Longmans, 1931, p. 267.) The question goes even further: whether Bismarck's achievements were not only, as Gooch implies, unconstructive as regards the future of Europe and humanity but even as regards Germany. In Germany, through Bismarck's successes, "the idolatry of the state reached its logical issue in the elevation of force to the sovereign principle in national life and in international relations" (*ibid.*, p. 230), and it was Treitschke, the "Bismarck of the chair" (*ibid.*, p. 155), who formed the mind of young Germany in the glorification of the right of the strong and in the hatred of France, liberalism, democracy, socialism, Catholics, and Jews.

Prussian reaction was supported by the Church. Prussia was practically a Lutheran theocracy. "Lutheranism of this type hallowed the realistic sense of power, and the ethical virtues of obedience, reverence, and respect for authority, which are indispensable to Prussian militarism. Thus Christianity and a conservative political attitude became identified with each other, as well as piety and love of power, purity of doctrine and the

glorification of war and the aristocratic standpoint." (Ernst Troeltsch, *The Social Teachings of
the Christian Churches*, translated by Olive Wyon,
New York: Macmillan, 1931, II, 575.) Ernst
Troeltsch also points out the great difference in the
attitude between the Lutheran church and the
Calvinist churches in the Anglo-Saxon countries,
in Switzerland and the Netherlands. Cf., on the
religious and philosophical background of German
history in the nineteenth and twentieth centuries,
Helmuth Plessner, *Das Schicksal deutschen Geistes
im Ausgang seiner bürgerlichen Epoche* (Zürich:
Niehans, 1935).

After the defeat in the World War the position
and prestige of the Prussian army seemed for a
short while dimmed, but with the election of
Marshal von Hindenburg to the Presidency of the
Republic in 1925 the symbolic value of the Prussian army was restored and the old Prussian tradition revived to full strength. Hindenburg as a
man and as a symbol (he became in 1932 the candi-
date of the "left" republican parties) paved the
way for the full-fledged return of the military
regime in 1933. Cf. Hermann Oncken's remarks
in his *Nation und Geschichte* (Berlin: Grote, 1935),
pp. 123–124, 130. The traditions of Frederick II,
of Scharnhorst and Gneisenau, of Bismarck and
Roon, were rekindled in Potsdam in 1933.

On the other hand, younger historians of our
day are more inclined to a favorable view of
Napoleon III. Robert C. Binkley believes that:

"In 1863 he was perhaps the last genuine European who stood in a place of authority, a successor to Metternich, a precursor of Woodrow Wilson. ... He visioned a Europe that would accept confederation in the various national areas, and defer to the authority of the concert as expressed in a Congress." (*Realism and Nationalism, 1852–1871*, New York: Harpers, 1935, pp. 260, 304.)

4. As far back as 1827 Goethe praised the United States in a brief poem, "Den Vereinigten Staaten."

> Amerika, du hast es besser
> Als unser Kontinent, das alte,
> Hast keine verfallene Schlösser
> Und keine Basalte.
> Dich stört nicht im Innern,
> Zu lebendiger Zeit,
> Unnützes Erinnern
> Und vergeblicher Streit.
>
> Benutzt die Gegenwart mit Glück!
> Und wenn nun eure Kinder dichten,
> Bewahre sie ein gut Geschick
> Vor Ritter-, Räuber- und Gespenster-
>   [geschichten.

("America, thou art more fortunate than our old continent. Thou hast no ruined castles, no venerable stones. No useless memories, no vain feuds harry thee in thy soul when thou wishest to live in the present. Make something happy out of today! And when thy children start to write, may a kind Providence preserve them from tales of knights, robbers, and ghosts.")

5. The phrase "nineteenth century" is used in these lectures to cover the period from the American and French revolutions to the World War.

6. The secularization of western humanity in the transition to the nineteenth century has been masterfully analyzed in Paul Hazard's *La Crise de la Conscience Européenne 1680–1715* (2 vols., Paris: Boivin et Cie, 1935) and in Bernhard Groethuysen's *Die Entstehung der bürgerlichen Welt- und Lebensanschauung in Frankreich* (2 vols., Halle: Niemeyer, 1927–30).

7. Carl Schmitt, *Der Begriff des Politischen*, 3d ed., Hamburg: Hanseatische Verlagsanstalt, 1933. Cf. the article by Hugo Fiala, "Politischer Dezisionismus," in *Revue Internationale de la Théorie du Droit* (Brno, Czechoslovakia), 1935, No. 2.

8. Adolf Hitler, *Mein Kampf* (Munich: Franz Eher, 1933), II, 438. The author speaks there of the fact that if the German people had possessed greater cohesion the German nation would then have achieved the domination of the world (Weltherrschaft). If the German nation had become the master of the globe (Herrin des Erdballs), then it would have established peace on earth. "Ein Friede, gestützt nicht durch die Palmwedel tränenreicher pazifistischer Klageweiber, sondern begründet durch das siegreiche

Schwert eines die Welt in den Dienst einer höheren Kultur nehmenden Herrenvolkes." Through National Socialism the German nation hopes to gain that cohesion which was missing.

9. The text of Signor Mussolini's article was made easily accessible in English in *International Conciliation*, No. 306 (New York: Carnegie Endowment for International Peace, January 1935).

10. *Complete Works of Friedrich Nietzsche*, edited by Oscar Levy (London: T. N. Foulis, 1903–13), vols. XIV–XV, Aphorisms 854–855.

11. Of the Prussian state and of the method of government it was the first to evolve and to bring to perfection in Europe, Lord Acton said: "Government so understood is the intellectual guide of the nation, the promoter of wealth, the teacher of knowledge, the guardian of morality, the mainspring of the ascending movement of man. That is the tremendous power supported by millions of bayonets, which . . . was developed . . . chiefly at Berlin; and it is the greatest danger that remains to be encountered by the Anglo-Saxon race." (*Lectures on Modern History*, London: Macmillan, 1906, p. 289.)

Although much in modern German nationalism is conditioned by the specific attitude of Lutheran Protestantism — entirely different from the attitude of Calvinism as well as of Catholicism — and by the Prussian tradition of the eighteenth century, the decisive factor seems to me to consist however in the fact that the national consciousness of the English and of the French peoples was awakened in revolutionary movements against domestic tyranny and injustice. Both movements, the English in the seventeenth and even more the French in the eighteenth century, carried a humanitarian appeal, a faith in reform and an enthusiasm for the "Kingdom of God." German national consciousness was awakened in the struggle against Napoleon, in a fight against an external enemy. The hatred for Napoleon coupled itself with an abhorrence of the principles for which he stood, the principles of the French Revolution, of equality and liberalism, of rationalism and cosmopolitan humanism. French nationalism developed from its basis in a liberal and democratic sense and asserted its principles in 1830, in 1848, in 1877, and since 1878 against all opposition from authoritarian and military circles. German nationalism developed on a basis opposed to "French ideas" and drew its inspiration from romanticism, which after 1815 regarded the "French ideas" as definitely defeated, as an infamous and unfortunate interlude in history, alien to the German spirit. The "French influences" in Germany, the liberalism of Young Germany and of the 1848 Republicans, were not strong enough to maintain themselves against romanticism and against the success of Prussianism under Bismarck.

12. The popularization of Darwin's theories achieved what had been begun in the eighteenth century. After the French Revolution religion,

disdained or neglected by the ruling classes and intellectuals in the eighteenth century, regained in many ways, at least socially, its position of respectability with the upper classes. Religion seemed able to justify the existing order. This belief that the *de facto* order is also the legitimate order because it has its roots in an authority which, viewed through man's inadequate eyes, is an irrational autocracy, found its classic expression in De Maistre's passage in *Les Soirées de Saint-Pétersbourg*, 8ᵉ Entretien: "Dieu étant une fois admis, et sa justice l'étant aussi comme un attribut nécessaire de la Divinité, le théiste . . . doit dire . . .: un tel ordre de choses a lieu sous l'empire d'un Dieu essentiellement juste, donc cet ordre de choses est juste pour des raisons que nous ignorons." ("Once the existence of God is admitted, and his justice as a necessary attribute of divinity, the theist must say: Such an order of things exists under the rule of an essentially just God; therefore this order of things is just for reasons of which we are ignorant.") (*Oeuvres de Joseph de Maistre*, Bruxelles: La Société Nationale pour la Propagation des Bons Livres, 1838, II, 99.) As against this attitude, Ludwig Feuerbach declared, in the third of his "Lectures on the Essence of Religion" which he delivered in Heidelberg at the time the Diet met at Frankfurt am Main, that he wished to transform "die Menschen aus Theologen zu Anthropologen, aus Theophilen zu Philanthropen, aus Candidaten des Jenseits zu Studenten des

Diesseits, aus religiösen und politischen Kammer-
dienern der himmlichen und irdischen Monarchie
und Aristokratie zu freien selbstbewussten Bür-
gern der Erde" ("to transform men from theolo-
gians into anthropologians ... from candidates for
the next world to students of this world, from
religious and political valets of the celestial and
terrestrial monarchy and aristocracy into free and
self-respecting citizens of the earth"). (*Vorlesun-
gen über das Wesen der Religion nebst Zusätzen und
Anmerkungen*, hg. von Wilhelm Bolin, Stuttgart:
Fr. Fromanns, 1908, pp. 28–29.)

Against De Maistre's irrationalism David Friedrich Strauss maintained in his *Streitschriften zur
Vertheidigung meiner Schrift über das Leben Jesu*
(Tübingen: Osiander, 1838, vol. I, part 2, p. 185):
"Nichts gilt mehr, weil es ist, sondern nur so weit
es sich als geltend ausweisen kann." ("Nothing is
valid because it exists, but only as far as its
validity can be proved.") Feuerbach and Strauss
attacked not only fundamentalism but the basis
of the divine right of kings and the privileges of
the aristocracy. The popularization of Darwin's
theory in the second half of the nineteenth century
completed the destruction of religious fundamentalism, but at the same time prepared the ground
for an undermining of the rational equality of man
by the proclamation of the natural inequality of
man. The sanction of religion was replaced by the
sanction of naturalistic science.

13. Cf. G. A. Borgese, "The Intellectual Ori-

gins of Fascism," in *Social Research* (New York), 1934, vol. I, no. 4 (November 1934), pp. 480–482. Croce's words are quoted from his *History of Italy, 1871–1915* (Oxford: The Clarendon Press, 1929), p. 240.

14. The cleavage between Western Europe, with its liberal and democratic traditions firmly rooted in the history of its nations and molding their political and social life, and Central and Eastern Europe with their autocratic and theocratic traditions, had found in the nineteenth century its expression in the international field in the efforts of the Hohenzollerns and of Bismarck to create an alliance between Russia, Prussia, and Austria as a firm bulwark for conservatism and against the danger of the penetration of liberal and democratic ideas from the West. The first treaty of alliance between Austria-Hungary, Germany, and Italy, concluded on May 20, 1882, declared the aim of the monarchs concluding the Triple Alliance to be "to fortify the monarchical principle and thereby to assure the unimpaired maintenance of the social and political order in their respective states" (Alfred Franzis Pribram, *The Secret Treaties of Austria-Hungary, 1879–1914*, Harvard University Press, 1920, I, 65). Even at the last prolongation of the Triple Alliance, in the treaty of December 5, 1912, the three monarchs declared themselves firmly "resolved to assure to their states the continuation of the benefits which the maintenance of the Triple Alliance guarantees to them, from the

political point of view as well as from the monarchical and social point of view" (*ibid.*, p. 245).
Bismarck, whose efforts had all been concentrated
on bringing about a permanent alliance among
the three eastern conservative empires, nevertheless agreed, although not with special eagerness, to
include Italy in his system of alliances, "to protect the Italian monarchy from the dangers which
must inevitably arise from an alliance by treaty
with France and from the reciprocal support of
the radical elements of France and Italy" (Instruction from the Foreign Office in Berlin to the
German Ambassador in Vienna, February 28,
1882; *ibid.*, II, 18).

The German historian Hans Delbrück stressed
in his *Regierung und Volkswille* (Berlin: Georg
Stilke, 1914, p. 59) that Parliaments came into
existence or into power in democratic countries
like France, England, America, and others, through
a struggle against traditional authority and by
overthrowing or defeating it; the German Reichs-
tag and the Prussian Landtag, however, were
created by the traditional authority. Therefore in
Germany the real power remained with the Monarchy through the army and the bureaucracy.
There are few more revealing passages than Delbrück's discussion of the position of the army in
democracies and in Germany (pp. 133–148). Even
a man of Delbrück's standing could not imagine
that the Allied armies in the approaching World
War could be victorious under the supreme control

of civilians, nay of democratic radicals like Cle-
menceau or Lloyd George. He expected that a victorious French army would put an end to the parlia-
mentary regime in France (p. 135). How little did
this great historian understand democratic nations
and traditions! Therefore he could seriously pro-
claim (p. 148): "Deutschland hat die demokrat-
ischeste aller Institutionen . . . die allgemeine
Wehrpflicht" ("Germany has the most democratic
of all institutions, general military conscription").

This cleavage of East and West in Europe has
grown since the World War. In France and England the pacifist tendencies in the population have
strongly increased. France has resumed the trend
towards the left which she has followed steadily
since 1879 and which, even overcoming the great
crises of the Boulanger and Dreyfus affairs, had re-
sulted before the World War in the victory of the
anti-militaristic, anti-clerical, pacifist, and reform-
ist forces. The elections in France after the World
War from 1924 onward and including that of 1936
have carried on this victorious trend of democracy,
notwithstanding the threatening example set by
some neighboring countries to the East. One of
the most astonishing factors in British policy since
the World War, in complete contradiction to the
pre-War attitude, is the influence of the growing
pacifist outlook of the population upon the government which made itself felt in almost all international moves from September, 1922, when the
government of Lloyd George had to resign on ac-

count of its bellicose attitude towards nationalist Turkey, down to the British concessions to Turkey and the Soviet Union in the negotiations on the Straits in July, 1936, which gave up the "interests" or "rights" for which Great Britain before the World War was ready to fight more than once.

In contrast to this pacifist attitude of the western democracies which try to arrive at settlements by compromise and moderation is the pronounced trend towards militarism and education in the war spirit in the countries east of the Rhine and the Alps and their resolution to settle disputes not by negotiation and compromise, but by action and by *faits accomplis*. As a logical consequence of this situation the initiative in international affairs has shifted during the last years more and more away from the Western European democracies.

The far-reaching differences between Western and German political thought which had always been stressed in Germany in the opposition of German romanticism to Western ideas are discussed by Ernst Troeltsch in an address delivered in Berlin in October, 1922, translated under the title, "The Ideas of Natural Law and Humanity in World Politics," in Appendix I to Otto Gierke's *Natural Law and the Theory of Society, 1500–1800*, translated by Ernest Barker (Cambridge University Press, 1934), I, 201–222. The same subject is discussed and the development of political ideas in the United States, in France, and in England as compared to the development in Germany is pointed out by Ernest Barker in his Introduction, pp. xlvi–lxxxvii.

15. Spengler, *Politische Schriften* (Munich: C. H. Beck, 1933), p. 105.

16. *Jahre der Entscheidung*: Part I, *Deutschland und die Weltgeschichtliche Entwicklung* (Munich: C. H. Beck, 1933), p. 63. On page 66 Spengler says that the more important a civilization is the more it resembles the formation of a noble animal or plant body.

17. *Ibid.,* p. 14.

18. *Ibid.,* p. 24.

19. Charles James Fox, *Speeches during the French Revolutionary War Period* (Everyman's Library, New York: E. P. Dutton, 1924), p. 194.

20. The first book on Kierkegaard in English has only recently been published — E. L. Allen, *Kierkegaard, His Life and Thought* (New York: Harpers, 1936). Since then the first English translation from Kierkegaard has appeared under the title *Philosophical Fragments, or, A Fragment of Philosophy* (Princeton: Princeton University Press for the American-Scandinavian Foundation, 1936). Of modern German theology there is a very good survey given by Paul Banwell Means, *Things That Are Caesar's, the Genesis of the German Church Conflict* (New York: Round Table Press, 1935). This book also contains a good and useful discussion of the background and the philosophy of the National Socialist movement.

On the theology of Karl Barth and on other modern theological movements and their attitude in the present situation see Edwin Ewart Aubrey, *Present Theological Tendencies* (New York: Harpers, 1936). Cf. also my *Martin Buber, sein Werk und seine Zeit, Ein Versuch über Religion und Politik* (Hellerau: Hegner; now Berlin: Schocken, 1929).

21. *Jahre der Entscheidung,* p. 12.

22. The phrase "Entzauberung der Welt" was first used by Max Weber in *Gesammelte Aufsätze zur Religionssoziologie* (Tübingen: Mohr, 1920), I, 263. In the same important essay, "Die Wirtschaftsethik der Weltreligionen," Weber distinguishes besides the rational authority of law charismatic and traditionalistic authority. He understands by charisma the uncommon (ausseralltäglich) quality of a man and his domination over other men by means of their faith in his exceptional possession of it. Their submission depends therefore upon manifestations of the magic power of the leader through success, victories, and generally upon the well-being of his followers. The recrudescence of charismatic leadership is characteristic in our time of Central Europe. By traditionalism, which we find in the Orient today struggling against modern civilization and which was general in Europe before the coming of modern civilization, he understands faith in the accustomed as the inviolable norm of our actions. (*Ibid.,* pp. 268 f.)

23. "Qu'est-ce que l'Europe? Une pensée qui ne se contente jamais. Sans pitié pour elle-même, elle ne cesse jamais de poursuivre deux quêtes — l'une vers le bonheur; l'autre qui lui est plus indispensable encore et plus chère, vers la vérité. A peine a-t-elle trouvé un état qui semble répondre à cette double exigence, elle s'aperçoit, elle sait qu'elle ne tient encore, d'une prise incertaine, que le provisoire, que le relatif: et elle recommence sa recherche désespérée qui fait sa gloire et son tourment." — II, 287.

24. A translation of Savigny's pamphlet by Abraham Hayward, *Of the Vocation of our Age for Legislation and Jurisprudence*, was printed by Littlewood and Co., London, 1831 (?), "Not for Sale." A copy of the book is in the Widener Library.

25. The book by Arthur, Comte de Gobineau, *Essai sur l'Inégalité des races humaines*, appeared in Paris in four volumes, 1853–55. The quotations from Nietzsche are from *The Will to Power*, Aphorisms 1005 and 462. Schopenhauer in his deep pessimism had denied the possibility of a happy life and resigned himself to the tragic fact of suffering. Nietzsche, however, glorifies the tragedy of life. In *The Will to Power*, Aphorism 1052, he opposes his Dionysian tragic sense to Christian suffering. In his case "existence itself is regarded as sufficiently holy to justify an enormous amount of suffering. The tragic man says 'yea' even to the most excruciating suffering: he is

sufficiently strong, rich, and capable of deifying to be able to do this."

26. These movements of intellectual and social unrest made themselves felt especially in those countries where the effects of the French Revolution and of democracy had not altered the traditional authoritarian structure of society. They were especially vehement in Germany. Stirred by metaphysics and music, torn by religious wars and lacking unity as did no other nation, suffering under the prevailing relics of a feudal and militaristic order, and since 1871 subjected to the relentless drive for material power, the youth of Germany developed a confused but consuming desire for a fuller and richer civilization which would integrate all strata of the population. Under similar conditions, similar movements made themselves felt in Russia and in Italy. The significance of the Youth Movements in the last years before the World War and immediately after the World War in the social and intellectual changes in Eastern Europe, and partly in Asia, has been analyzed in the article "Youth Movements" in the *Encyclopedia of the Social Sciences*, vol. XV.

27. In a similar way Gabriele d'Annunzio had sent out his famous drama, *La Nave*, which in glorification of the past history of Venice demanded Italy's mastery of the sea, especially the Adriatic, in 1908 with the famous verse, "Arma la prora e salpa verso il mondo" ("Arm the prow

and sail towards the world!"), which again implies a march or a sailing without any very clear direction.

28. Science has become, as much as economics, a *potentiel de guerre*. How far science has been nationalized was revealed at the five hundred and fiftieth anniversary of the University of Heidelberg in the summer of 1936, when, on the façade of a building built and presented by Americans to the University, the statue of Pallas Athene as a classic head of the Republic of Letters was replaced by the German eagle, and the inscription "To the eternal spirit" by the nationalistic "To the German spirit."

This tendency towards the nationalization of science is to be found not only in the social sciences, but also in natural sciences and in mathematics, which until very recently had been regarded as the bulwark of objective rationalism. In January, 1936, a new bi-monthly started publication under the title *Deutsche Mathematik*, edited on behalf of the Deutsche Forschungsgemeinschaft and commencing with the invocation of a word of *Der Führer*. In the preface to the first issue we read: "Wir dienen der deutschen Art in der Mathematik und wollen sie pflegen. Wir sind nicht allein auf dieser Welt: Andere Völker haben den gleichen Anspruch auf die Auswirkung ihrer Eigenart in der mathematischen Betätigung. Mannigfache Berührung besteht zwischen der mathematischen Arbeit der verschiedenen Völker. Für die Anregung und Belehrung, die sich daraus auch für uns ergibt, hat unsere Zeitschrift einen offenen Blick. Doch sehen wir alles unter den Gesichtspunkten der mathematischen Leistung unseres Volkes. Ihr gilt unsere Arbeit, eingedenk der Tatsache, dass auch mathematisches Schaffen sich um so kräftiger entfaltet und damit auch zu um so grösserer Bedeutung für die Mitwelt gelangt, je tiefer es in einem Volkstum verwurzelt ist." ("We serve the German way in mathematics and wish to cultivate it. We are not alone in this world: other peoples have the same claim to express their way in mathematics. Various points of contact exist between the mathematical work of the different peoples. Our review has an open mind for the suggestions and information which may derive therefrom for us, also. But we see everything from the standpoint of the mathematical accomplishments of our people. For it our labor is meant, conscious of the fact that creative mathematics also develops the stronger and achieves the greater importance for the world the deeper it is rooted in the national spirit.") How far the mathematical articles in the review express a specific German spirit I am certainly not competent to judge, but of greatest interest for the historian of our civilization will be the introductory general articles like that by Professor Erhard Tornier of Göttingen, who attacks vehemently "jüdisch-liberalistisches Denken" in mathematics as opposed to the "deutsche völkische Wissenschaft" which is the goal aimed at.

29. Only one hundred years ago John C. Calhoun could defend slavery and could point out that there never has existed a wealthy and civilized society without slavery. "But let me not be understood as admitting even by implication that the existing relations between the two races in the slave holding states is an evil; — far otherwise, I hold it to be a good as it has thus far proved to be to both and will continue to prove so if not disturbed by the fell spirit of abolition." (Speech on Reception of Abolition Petitions, February 6, 1837, *Works of John C. Calhoun*, edited by Richard K. Crallé, New York, 1853, II, 630.) Cf. also Jeannette Reid Tandy, "Pro-Slavery Propaganda in American Fiction in the Fifties," in the *South Atlantic Quarterly*, XXI, 41–50, 170–178 (1922). A good selection of pro-slavery arguments is given in a publication, *The Pro-Slavery Argument; as Maintained by the Most Distinguished Writers of the Southern States, Containing the Several Essays, on the Subject, of Chancellor Harper, Governor Hammond, Dr. Simms, and Professor Dew* (Charleston, 1852). Chancellor William Harper began his essay as follows: "The institution of domestic slavery exists over far the greater portion of the inhabited earth. Until within a very few centuries, it may be said to have existed over the whole earth — at least in all those portions of it which had made any advances towards civilization. We might safely conclude then, that it is deeply founded in the nature of man and the

exigencies of human society." Professor Thomas
Roderick Dew, professor of history, metaphysics,
and political law at the College of William and
Mary, concluded his very long, able, and scholarly
essay on the abolition of slavery with the following
sentences: "Once more do we call upon our statesmen to pause, ere they engage in this ruinous
scheme. The power of man has limits, and he
should never attempt impossibilities. . . . The deep
and solid foundations of society cannot be broken
up by the vain fiat of the legislator. . . . Let us reflect on these things, and learn wisdom from experience; and know that the relation of society,
generated by the lapse of ages, cannot be altered
in a day." The same wisdom is presented to us today, no longer in connection with the abolition of
slavery, but in connection with the abolition of
war or the abolition of sovereign national states.
We do not know much about the "nature" of
man, but we know that political ideas and social
institutions change.

30. "C'est précisément parce que la force des
choses tend toujours à détruire l'égalité que la
force de la législation doit toujours tendre à la
maintenir." — J. J. Rousseau, *Du Contrat Social*,
edited by Georges Beaulavon (3d ed., Paris:
Rieder, 1922), Book II, chapter xi, p. 202. Cf.
also the last sentence of chapter ix in Book I.

31. The nineteenth century produced a deep
change in the psychology of the masses, in their
claim to equality. This change was entirely due to

the penetration of the political ideas of the nineteenth century to the masses, a penetration which happened very frequently against the will of the upper classes but which could not be impeded, as the liberty and equality proclaimed by the new ideas were in theory not confined to those classes or races which wished to monopolize and to exploit them. J. L. and Barbara Hammond describe in *The Town Labourer, 1760–1832* (London: Longmans, 1920, p. 288) the change in the psychology of the English working man under the influence of the ideas of the French Revolution, in a memorable passage:

"When the French Revolution broke out there was no resemblance between the spirit of the working classes in the north and the Midlands, and the spirit of the Paris democrat, on fire with vivid and emancipating enthusiasms. The English working classes in the centres of the new industry were conservative, insular, Philistine. Manchester, like Birmingham, was predominantly Church and King; and nobody who reads Bamford's description of the treatment his father and his father's friends received at Middleton will make the mistake of supposing that the Reformers whom Pitt persecuted were dangerous to the State by reason of their popularity. The working classes, as a body, in the north and the Midlands were profoundly indifferent to ideas or causes. So long as they could drink, watch a cock-fight or bull-baiting or horse-race, and earn a reasonable living, they were contented as the squires whose tastes, if rather more expensive, were in kind not dissimilar. No visions exalted or disturbed their souls, and the *sans-culottes* of Bolton or Wigan were as ready as the parsons or the squires to put anybody who talked or looked like a French Jacobin into the nearest and darkest horsepond.

"By the end of our period a great change had come over the working classes. They had become what Pitt and Castlereagh tried so hard to prevent them from becoming, politicians. They talked about the affairs of the State: they discussed the basis of rights and duties, they took an ominous interest in taxes and sinecures, and it was not the phrases of 1789 but the cry of Church and King that awakened their execrations. All the efforts of civilization seemed to have been made in vain when the one question that absorbed the minds of the factory workers as they poured from the mills was the question whether Cobbett's *Political Register* had come with the latest coach."

Victor Hugo expressed this change in the psychology of the masses in his famous speech in the Assemblée Legislative on July 9, 1849. "L'homme du peuple aujourd'hui souffre avec les sentiments doubles et contradictoires de sa misère résultant du fait et de sa grandeur résultant du droit." ("The man in the masses suffers today with the two-fold and contradictory feeling of his actual misery and of the greatness to which he knows himself entitled.")

It is this awakening of the masses to the claims of equality and happiness, of liberty and dignity, which is the remarkable fact of the nineteenth century among the white races and of the twentieth century in Asia and Africa. The fight of the masses for their emancipation is still very far from being achieved, but nevertheless what a difference from the situation before the French Revolution! Then and even far into the nineteenth century the right to happiness for the masses was not recognized. Happiness was reserved to the upper classes; to everybody only a certain graded happiness was due according to his station in life; and this situation was generally accepted. The abolition of the privileges of aristocracy was deemed unthinkable, and Edmund Burke characterized this system of privileges as "the result of profound reflection, or rather the happy effect of following nature, which is wisdom without reflection, and above it" (*Reflections on the French Revolution*, Everyman's Library, p. 31). Nature has since apparently changed or has been accepted as changing, not only in democratic France but even in aristocratic England. (Cf. on that question Leonard Woolf, *After the Deluge, A Study of Communal Psychology*, vol. I, New York Harcourt, Brace, & Co., 1931.) Burke also believed that with the disappearance of the political privileges of aristocracy and clergy, "along with its natural protectors and guardians, learning will be cast into the mire, and trodden down under the hoofs of a swinish multitude" (*op. cit.*, p. 76).

32. Carl Schmitt speaks in his *Der Begriff des Politischen*, p. 56, of the nineteenth century as "dieses mit Illusion und Betrug angefüllten Säculums" ("this century full of illusion and fraud"). A similar position was taken by Vilfredo Pareto, who, having lost faith in the ideals of the nineteenth century, tried to unmask them as mendacious ideologies for instinctive desires. His resentful cynicism is a characteristic expression of the nihilism of some thinkers during and since the World War period. Cf. Leopold v. Wiese, "Vilfredo Pareto als Soziologe," in *Zeitschrift für Nationalökonomie* (Vienna: Julius Springer), vol. VII, No. 4, pp. 433 ff. (December 1936), and Ellsworth Faris, "An Estimate of Pareto," in *American Journal of Sociology*, XLI, 657 ff. (March 1936).

33. It may be noted here that whereas Fascism and Communism agree in their cult of force, Communism is a strictly rationalist doctrine. Notwithstanding many outward resemblances and their similarly totalitarian character, Communist and Fascist dictatorships are opposite as regards their aims and their philosophies of life. Fascism in all its forms is nationalistic and militaristic: it regards the expansion of the nation as an essential manifestation of vitality, and the willing acceptance of the risks that war implies as a noble way of life. It believes in the immutable and beneficial inequality of men, nations, and races. Communism is supranational and cosmopolitan. It believes in the equality of men, nations, and races.

It aims professedly at the creation of a society of free individuals living in security and peaceful coöperation. Fascism with its glorification of the strong state and the natural inequality of men believes in authority and leadership as an essential and immutable foundation. Communism professedly regards dictatorship as a transitory phenomenon towards an absolute democracy, the abolition of the state, and the establishment of a world-wide community of free individuals. Fascism trusts in the charisma of a superman who by mystic identification embodies and represents the nation. Communism trusts in a rational system of social philosophy and interpretation of history. Fascism working upon the emotions and the historical memories of a particular nation is intrinsically bound up with the past. Rational Communism declares its methods and results of universal applicability and is concerned entirely with the future, to which it sacrifices not only the past but even the present. Fascism has no high opinion of liberalism, equality, and individual liberty. Communism professes that in the future socialist society, should it ever emerge, all the achievements of liberalism — freedom of conscience and thought, of expression and association, equality of all individuals without distinction of sex or race, equal opportunity for everybody and equal access to the sources of knowledge and science — will be realized. Cf. my article "Communist and Fascist Dictatorship, a Comparative Study," in *Dictator-*

ship in the Modern World, edited by Guy Stanton Ford (University of Minnesota Press, 1935), pp. 141–160.

34. In a strict sense the word Imperialism can also be employed for the relation of dominating peoples to subject European peoples — which are generally the more backward ones — as for instance the relations between English and Irish, Prussians and Poles, Russians and Ukrainians. The difference, however, is that in the European countries at the end of the nineteenth century at least complete legal equality had been established between the dominating and the subject races, although no social, economic, or cultural equality.

A recent discussion of the origins of modern imperialism is contained in William L. Langer's *The Diplomacy of Imperialism, 1890–1902* (New York: A. A. Knopf, 1935), I, 67–100, and in his article "A Critique of Imperialism," in *Foreign Affairs* (New York), vol. XIV, no. 1, pp. 102–119 (October 1935). An excellent discussion of the present-day problems of imperialism in Africa is given in the Burge Memorial Lecture *Africa and Peace* by A. G. Fraser (Oxford: Clarendon Press, 1936).

On imperialism in Asia and Africa and on the nefarious effects which imperialism had not only on the inhabitants of those countries but also on democracy and peace in Europe, Kant has already said in his *Zum Ewigen Frieden*, Dritter Definitivartikel : "If we compare the barbarian instances of inhospitality referred to with the inhuman behaviour of the civilised, and especially the commercial, States of our Continent, the injustice practised by them in their first contact with foreign lands and peoples, fills us with horror, the mere *visiting* of such peoples being regarded by them as equivalent to a *conquest*. America, the Negro Lands, the Spice Islands, the Cape of Good Hope, etc., on being discovered, were treated as countries that belonged to nobody; for the Aboriginal inhabitants were reckoned as nothing. In the East Indies, under the pretext of intending merely to plant commercial settlements, the Europeans introduced foreign troops, and with them oppression of the Natives, instigation of the different States to widespread wars, famine, sedition, perfidy, and all the litany of evils that can oppress the human race.... The worst (or, regarded from the standpoint of a moral judge, the best) of all this is that no satisfaction is derived from this violence, as all these commercial Societies are at present on the verge of ruin. The Sugar Islands — that seat of the cruellest and completest slavery — have offered up no real profit, but have been only indirectly of account, and that in no praiseworthy relation. They have only furnished sailors for ships of war, and have thereby contributed to the carrying on of wars in Europe. And all this has been done by nations who make a great ado about their piety, and who, while drinking up iniquity like water, would have themselves regarded as the very elect of the orthodox Faith."

(Translated by W. Hastie in *Kant's Principles of Politics*, Edinburgh: Clark, 1891, pp. 102–103.)

35. A leading British economist, Professor T. E. Gregory, draws from the realization of these facts the following sagacious conclusions: "Whatever the causal sequence may be, it is clear that we should view the Eastern scene in the light of our own historical experience and recognize that the ultimate condition for a rise in the Eastern standard of life is such a balance between population growth and technical progress as to permit of a surplus which will raise the per capita welfare of Eastern population. The attainment of this surplus . . . is only possible by means of industrialization. . . . A growing population with growing resources represents a growing market: in fact, the East is reproducing the conditions which made for the most rapid economic growth in other parts of the world in a not very remote past. . . . There is no lack of a market, in the sense that there is an insufficient number of potential consumers; what is lacking is the means to satisfy their requirements given the existing productivity. To raise their standards it is necessary to increase productive equipment — and that is to industrialize. . . . An expansion of production over a large part of the world, accompanied by expanding population and a rising standard of life, is not fundamentally inconsistent with the continued well-being of the rest of the world, or, indeed, with the growth of that well-being. But it does not in the least

follow from this that such a development may not be permanently inimical to particular functions of the non-Eastern world, or that this development may not involve great problems of inter-adjustment which, until they have taken place, may prove to be inimical to large portions of the non-Eastern world. . . . Industrialization is the only possible solution for the appalling absolute standards of life in the East. . . . It follows that, difficult as the problems of adjustment may be, they remain subsidiary, not in the sense that solutions are easy to find, but in the sense that they flow from an historical process which cannot be resisted, and which ought not to be resisted." (Conclusion, by T. E. Gregory, to *Eastern Industrialization and its Effect on the West*, by G. E. Hubbard, Oxford University Press, 1935, pp. 364, 365, 367, 371.)

36. David Hume, *Essays, Literary, Moral, and Political* (London: Ward, Lock & Co., no date), p. 23.

37. The books by Subhas Chandra Bose, *The Indian Struggle* (London: Wishart, 1935), and Jawaharlal Nehru, *An Autobiography with Musings on Recent Events in India* (London: John Lane, 1936), reflect the spirit of young Asia. Nehru says on page 420: "If we claim independence today it is with no desire for isolation. On the contrary we are perfectly willing to surrender part of that independence, in common with other countries, to a real international order." See in Nehru's book

especially chapter liv, "The Record of British Rule," and chapter lxii, "Paradoxes." The latter chapter ends: "We have managed to tie ourselves up into a number of knots, and it is difficult to get on till we untie them. That release will not come emotionally. What is better, Spinoza asked long ago: freedom through knowledge and understanding, or emotional bondage? He preferred the former."

38. It is the racial attitude of the white race which creates the "colored danger." By treating all non-white races with the same disdainful attitude, and by the claim which is frequently only implicitly made to rule and to exploit them, the whites as a "white danger" force the non-whites into a "united front." This feeling of racial superiority is of recent origin with the white races. In the Middle Ages neither the Crusaders nor Marco Polo had that feeling of superiority towards the non-whites. Ernst Kantorowicz says of Frederick II: "Unstinted admiration of the Arab mind was the weightiest factor with the Hohenstaufen Emperor. For Frederick II lived in a day when the East was the source of all European knowledge and science, as Italy and Roman culture were to the barbarian North, as of old the art and philosophy of Hellas were to Italy. . . . In all the anecdotes and reported conversations . . . one recurring note is the immense admiration and reverence . . . felt by this greater Emperor for the Muslim princes — himself almost sole arbiter

of the West. . . . All indications point to the fact that for the only time in his life, now vis-à-vis the East, Kaiser Frederick felt himself to be the learner and the gainer. . . . In his intercourse with Easterners Frederick displayed the gratitude which the Pope used to demand from him in vain. Only from the East did Frederick in fact receive new ideas and intellectual stimulus." (*Frederick the Second, 1194–1250*, translated by E. O. Lorimer, New York: Richard R. Smith, 1931, pp. 192, 195, 196.)

On the origins and implications of race feeling, see Arnold J. Toynbee, *A Study of History* (Oxford University Press, 1934), I, 207–249, 465–467. He believes that the race feeling engendered "by the English Protestant version of our western culture became the determining factor in the development of race feeling of western society as a whole. This has been a misfortune for mankind, for the Protestant temper and attitude and conduct in regard to race, as in many other vital issues, is inspired largely by the Old Testament; and in matters of race the promptings of this old-fashioned Syriac oracle are very clear and very savage." The English Protestants identified themselves with the old Israelites and the natives with the Canaanites whom the Lord had delivered into the hands of his chosen people to be destroyed or subjugated (pp. 211 f.). "Of course the fanaticism and ferocity of the race feeling which the Old Testament once instilled into Protestant souls have

both considerably abated as Protestantism itself
has evolved through Rationalism towards Agnosti-
cism" (p. 214). But then naturalistic and biological selection took the place of religious selection.
About the implications of race conflict in our time
and its growing acuteness, cf. the article on "Race
Conflict" in the *Encyclopedia of the Social Sciences*, vol. XIII.

39. A well-documented discussion of this im-
portant question is presented in Denna Frank
Fleming's *The United States and the League of
Nations, 1918–1920* (New York: Putnam, 1932).

40. The League of Nations could end the prevailing anarchy in the international order only if it
would become to a certain extent a super-state,
that is if the nations would give up part of their
sovereignty to the new international body. It is
sovereignty which conditions international anarchy, as it leads to the coexistence of completely independent and isolated units centered only in
their own interests and responsible to nobody
except themselves. This anarchic state becomes
increasingly dangerous with the growing interdependence of all nations. But all nations cling today with an undiminished tenacity to the political
doctrine of sovereignty. It is entirely useless to
blame one particular nation more than another
for the non-realization of the idea underlying the
League of Nations. Only collective security can
prevent war. Should there exist a system of collective security nobody would think of starting

wars. Instead of isolated nations we should have a society where each stands for all and all for each. If it were to be really enforced in a new spirit, no more would be needed than what is contained in the present very much attenuated text of the Covenant which was born of many compromises but which sets forth that an aggressor "shall *ipso facto* be deemed to have committed an act of war against" all other nations, which shall then "undertake immediately to subject it to a severance of all trade or financial relations, the prohibition of all intercourse...." Then the weak as well as the strong would feel secure, then fear and distrust would diminish and disarmament and peaceful readjustments of land and economic resources could become a reality. To claim disarmament without any real League of Nations and with the anarchy of sovereign states continuing must remain a pathetic but unrealistic sentimentalism.

If the League of Nations does not function and if the old sovereignty continues, bi-lateral treaties of friendship will certainly not be of any avail. Ethiopia was invaded and annexed by Italy not only in contravention of the Covenant of the League of Nations but also in contradiction to the treaty of amity, conciliation, and arbitration concluded between Italy and Ethiopia on August 2, 1928, for twenty years and reaffirmed by both countries on September 29, 1934. A very revealing book by Emilio de Bono, who directed the first operations in Italy's war against Ethiopia, *La*

Preparazione e le Primi Operazioni (Rome: Istituto Nazionale Fascista di Cultura, 1936), states plainly that Mussolini had prepared the war as far back as in 1933 and by the end of 1934 had laid down the detailed plans of aggression. He would never have dared to carry on the preparations so openly in 1935 had he believed in the strength of collective security. Collective security would do away with the danger of war. The defense forces of a collective security system would not only prevent aggression without being called forth for action, but they would not be surrounded by that emotional halo which surrounds, in the age of nationalism and national sovereignty, all national defense forces and defense problems.

An international order could, however, be realized only with the relinquishing of the idea of national sovereignty and with the complete equality of all peoples. With the new feeling of security and equality nationalism would decrease and lose all its aggressive and exclusive features of today. All that seems to belong to a distant future. "The more one studies history, the more astonishing does it seem that man, who is after all a rational animal, should have invented and passionately maintained the fantastic political institutions and political beliefs which have existed in all ages and have frequently been the causes of some of the worst of human catastrophes." (Leonard Woolf, *op. cit.*, p. 120.) But communal psychology changes fast and may further change

as a consequence of further deluges or the threats
of further deluges.

41. *Op. cit.*, p. 199.

42. The number of examples of psychological,
social, and political changes brought about during the last one hundred years against all the ex-
pectations of contemporaries, even very learned
and distinguished men who were reputed progressive in their days, could be multiplied endlessly. In 1807 Davies Giddy (called later Gil-
bert), afterwards President of the Royal Society, a
man of scientific attainments and a great patron
of scientific enterprise, opposed a bill for the
general provision of elementary schools throughout England. His argument runs: "However
specious in theory the project might be, of giving
education to the labouring classes of the poor, it
would in effect be found to be prejudicial to their
morals and happiness; it would teach them to de-
spise their lot in life, instead of making them good
servants in agriculture, and other laborious em-
ployments to which their rank in society had
destined them; instead of teaching them subordination, it would render them factious and
refractory, as was evident in the manufacturing
counties; it would enable them to read seditious
pamphlets, vicious books, and publications against
Christianity; it would render them insolent to
their superiors; and in a few years the result
would be that the legislature would find it necessary to direct the strong arm of power towards

them, and to furnish the executive magistrate with much more vigorous laws than were now in force." (J. L. and Barbara Hammond, *The Town Labourer*, p. 57.)

Even in 1847, education in England for the masses was no better than it is today in most Oriental countries.   On April 19 of that year Macaulay said, in a speech on education in the House of Commons: "Of eight thousand prisoners who had passed through Maidstone jail only fifty could read and write well. Turn from the registers of prisoners to the register of marriages. You will find that about a hundred and thirty thousand couples were married in the year 1844. Nearly one third of the men and nearly one half of the women, who are in the prime of life ... cannot write their own names. Remember that ... people may write their own names and yet have very little knowledge. Tens of thousands who were able to write their names had in all probability received only the wretched education of a common day school. We know what such a school too often is; a room crusted with filth ... the only machinery of instruction a dog-eared spelling book and a broken slate; the masters the refuse of all other callings ... men who cannot write a common letter without blunders, men who do not know whether Jerusalem is in Asia or America." (*Miscellanies*, by Lord Macaulay, Boston: Houghton, Mifflin, 1920, vol. I — Cambridge Edition of the Complete Writings, vol. IX — pp. 487–488.) That even today the educational facilities for the masses are inadequate in England and probably in many other countries is maintained by a London correspondent in *The New Republic* (New York), July 22, 1936, p. 315. "Social inequality in the distribution of educational opportunities exists on a scale that exceeds the wildest guesses of irresponsible agitators. . . . It is not mystical egalitarianism to demand the equalization of social opportunities. The mystics are those who deny the possibility of social improvement except by the aristocratic device of selective breeding. The choice that confronts us is between an uncertain and unskillful eugenic program and the highly successful methods of nineteenth century public hygiene, which have enormously raised the expectation of human life and physical welfare. The task of public psychological hygiene is to promote, through the control of our institutional environment, the maximum utilization of the talents and abilities of mankind."

43. *Critical, Historical, and Miscellaneous Essays* by Lord Macaulay (New York: 1860), II, 185, 186. Macaulay himself, in his speech on the People's Charter on May 3, 1842, regarded the granting of universal suffrage then as the greatest calamity ("If you grant that, the country is lost"), but with his views on education ("what we are asked to do is to give universal suffrage before there is universal education") he could foresee a day, distant in 1842, when universal suffrage could be "safely" granted.

44. This necessity was pointed out by Kant. He says in his *Die Idee zu einer allgemeinen Geschichte in weltbürgerlicher Absicht* (7. Satz): "Nature . . . works through wars, through the strain of never relaxed preparation for them, and through the necessity which every State is at least compelled to feel within itself, even in the midst of peace, to begin some imperfect efforts to carry out her purpose. And, at last, after many devastations, overthrows, and even complete internal exhaustion of their powers, the nations are driven forward to the goal which Reason might have well impressed upon them, without so much sad experience. This is none other than the advance out of the lawless state of savages and the entering into a Federation of Nations. It is thus brought about that every State, including even the smallest, may rely for its safety and its rights, not on its own power or its own judgment of Right, but only on this great International Federation, on its combined power, and on the decision of the common will according to laws. However visionary this idea may appear to be — and it has been ridiculed . . . it is nevertheless the inevitable issue of the necessity in which men involve one another. For this necessity must compel the Nations to the very resolution — however hard it may appear — to which the savage in his uncivilised state, was so unwillingly compelled, when he had to surrender his brutal liberty and seek rest and security in a Constitution regulated

by law." (Translated by W. Hastie, *op. cit.*, pp. 16–17.)

Of all the German thinkers, Kant was nearest to the Western European ideas of natural rights and humanity. (It is noteworthy that the three greatest Germans of modern times, Kant, Goethe, and Beethoven, belonged all three to the pre-nationalistic period of Germany. Beethoven admired republican and cosmopolitan France and his Ninth Symphony is the greatest hymn to humanity and fraternal equality, Goethe admired Napoleon in the fight against whom German nationalism arose under Prussian leadership, and had little understanding or liking for patriotism or of "Deutschtümelei.") German intellectual and with it social and political development did not follow Kant but the post-Kantians — Fichte, Hegel, and the Romanticists. Some elements of the rational ethicism of Kant and of the Enlightenment survived in Fichte and Hegel; they were lost in Bismarck's *Machtstaat.* The foremost sociological thinker of Germany before the World War, Max Weber, said in his lecture "Der Nationalstaat und die Volkswirtschaftspolitik" (1895), in which he made a plea for economic nationalism and economics as a *potentiel de guerre*: "Nicht Frieden und Menschenglück haben wir unseren Nachfahren mit auf den Weg zu geben, sondern den ewigen Kampf um die Erhaltung und Emporzüchtung unserer nationalen Art.... Die Machtinteressen der Nation sind, wo sie in Frage gestellt sind, die letzten

und entscheidenden Interessen, in deren Dienst
ihre Wirtschaftspolitik sich zu stellen hat.... Der
Nationalstaat ist uns die weltliche Machtorgani-
sation der Nation und in diesem Nationalstaat ist
für uns der letzte Wertmasstab auch der volks-
wirtschaftlichen Betrachtung die Staatsraison."
("It is not our task to pass on to our descendants
for their life journey peace and human happiness,
but the eternal struggle for the maintenance and
enhancement of our national way.... The power
and interests of the nation, where they are
questioned, are the last and decisive interests
which economic policy has to serve.... The
national state is for us the secular power organization of the nation and in this national state the
raison d'état is for us the ultimate yardstick for
economic considerations.") (*Gesammelte Politische
Schriften*, Munich: Drei Masken Verlag, 1921,
p. 20.)

It should be pointed out that in the last years
before the World War, simultaneously with the
growth of the Social Democratic Party which in
Germany represented for the masses of its voters
less a revolutionary Marxism than Western democratic thought and an opposition to Prussian
aristocratic militarism, there were some tendencies
of a return to the ideas of the Enlightenment.
Wilhelm Dilthey asked (in *Das Erlebnis und die
Dichtung*, Leipzig: Teubner, 1912, p. 174): "Ob
wir nicht manches von dem zurückholen müssen,
was wir von den Idealen der Aufklärung aufgegeben

haben?" ("Must we not regain some of the ideas of the Enlightenment which we have abandoned?") More prophetic even were the words of Wilhelm Windelband (*Die Philosophie im deutschen Geistes-leben des XIX. Jahrhunderts*, Tübingen: Mohr, 1909, p. 94): "In vielen Dingen sind wir heut-zutage in der Lage, für die Errungenschaften der Aufklärung an Klarheit und Freiheit des Lebens noch einmal in den Kampf, vielleicht in einen schwereren Kampf treten zu müssen, als die Aufklärung ihn siegreich bestanden hat." ("In many ways we are today in a situation in which we must resume the fight for the achievements of the Enlightenment in clarity and liberty of life, perhaps a more difficult struggle than that which the Enlightenment successfully waged.")

INDEX

INDEX

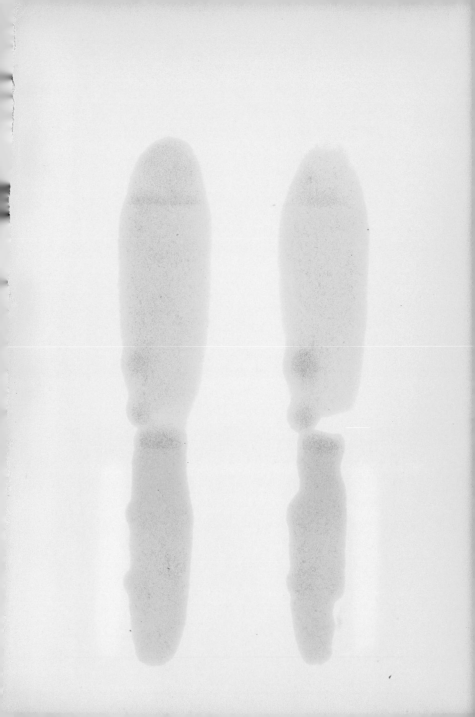